Python 3

The Ultimate Beginners Guide for Python 3 Programming

Preface

You have taken a crucial step in enriching yourself. Learning a new language is always difficult. More so, if it's a computer programming language. You have to start from scratch and slowly learn the basics.

However, the reward for your effort after your activity would be numerous. You can compare this experience to learning how to ride the bicycle. You may suffer minor accidents, but you will benefit from it eventually.

I have simplified the language and the explanations in this book - as much as possible - to help you, the beginner, grasp the basics of Python 3 programming. There are several examples, as well, to allow you to assimilate the concept.

Also, your correct mental attitude and optimism can help in providing you with a fun and fruitful learning experience.

Thanks again for downloading this book, I hope you enjoy it!

Table of content

Chapter 1: Introduction to Python 3

Python is a programming language used for interactive, portable and flexible programs. It has a syntax that can easily interface with other systems. It's object-oriented, meaning, it focuses on object-oriented data, modules and classes. You can use it for general purposes in programming. It has also a broad range of standard library that allows you to work quickly and more reliably.

The first versions of Python are the 2x series, which is still very useful even with the advent of the 3x series, because its features are compatible with more applications and systems. Because of some updates, the Python 3 series is still not accepted by other devices. There are some systems that are not adjusted to Python 3.

Nevertheless, Python 3 is the latest series of the Python programming language. Just like Python 2, it's easier to learn than most programming languages because its syntax is clear and simple and not difficult, unlike the statically typed languages.

Python has also an interactive interpreter, such as IDLE to allow learners to code quickly and check -at the moment - if their syntaxes are correct.

For this book, we will be focusing on the Python 3 series.

How to Install Python 3

You can easily install Python 3, by visiting directly the Python official website, www.python.org and download from there.

Find the corresponding installer to your device. Click download, then click Save File, and install your downloaded Python 3 in your computer. Be sure to remember where you stored it.

Click on your saved Python 3, and then Run it. The program itself will guide you through your installation.

After installation, you can open now the program to start using it. Choose the interpreter option with the GUI (Graphical User Interface).

This will open a shell, where you can start typing your codes. The shell is a small, square box, where you can input your Python statements.

Some computers come with an already installed Python programming language. You can check if Python is installed in your computer or device through your search box.

Steps in running Python on Windows:

Step #1 – Start your interpreter

Before you can execute or run commands, you must first set up your Python interpreter. You can quickly access your Python by typing Python in your command window. You could also type the path url of your Python file directly.

Step #2 – Enter your commands

After the interpreter shell appears, the prompt will start blinking. These are three arrows found at the left upper hand of the shell. You can now start typing your commands, and then wait for the interpreter to compile and execute them. The first statement is executed first and then the rest follows in chronological order.

Step #3 – Save needed files

You can start saving your Python files, after you have created them. The Python shell will not save your data, unless you purposely save them as .py files. Double check that your files are .py files before closing your shell.

Reminders:

- The prompt, three arrows >>>, will indicate that you, as the user, has to input something. As soon as you press 'enter', the return statement appears, so use the editor instead.

- The Python interpreter has an essential role in interpreting your data. If your syntax is incorrect, it will return an error, and indicate what error was committed.

- The hash tag, #, indicates that the statement following it is a comment, and is not part of the Python statement/code. This is used by coders to write their observations and notations for a particular statement.

- Python statements are usually enclosed by single or double quotes, and strings are enclosed in single or double quotes too, EXCEPT integers or numbers.

- The items inside the string are separated by commas. The commas denote that they are different from each other, and must be treated individually.

- You can access your strings by calling out their file names. But first, you must assign variables to them, so they can be tagged. With their tags, you can promptly retrieve them.

Working on your Python language is like studying your English language, you have to learn the correct grammar, to be able to construct proper Python syntaxes.

Chapter 2: Differences of Python 3 from Python 2

There are some differences of Python 2 from Python 3. If you want to know which one is recommended for you, you will have to consider your purpose for using it, and which among the two Python versions can work well with your device.

Python 3 is recommended because it has solved the problems encountered in Python 2.

To help you more in working with your Python 3, here are some differences you can expect.

Features of Python 3 that are different from Python 2

1. Print function

In Python 3, print is a function. So, when the print function is called, the object must be enclosed in parentheses. If not, it will return an error.

Example:

> >>>print "Hi, I'm Dave."
> Syntax Error: invalid syntax

You have to use parentheses for the correct command to be executed.

Example:

> >>>print ("Hi, I'm Dave.")
> Hi, I'm Dave.

This is not true with Python 2. Even without the parentheses, Python 2 will execute the command. Thus, you can also use the parentheses in Python 2, and it will still print the values or items. You can say that in this case, Python 2 has the advantage, because it's not sensitive to the absence or presence of the parentheses.

Nonetheless, Python 3 wins with regards to shorter codes, easier manipulations of data, and more relevant programs.

Example:

>>>*print "Hi, I'm Dave."* #This is not enclosed in parentheses, but Python 2 will print it. See result below:

Hi, I'm Dave.

2. super()

You can now call super() without arguments. This facilitates the process of single-inheritance, significantly. Python has this significant feature that's a huge advantage over Python 2.

3. Byte classes/Unicode

In Python 3, there are 2 byte classes (bytearrays and byte), while in Python 2, there are no byte types.

In Python 3, text and binary data is used. This is a change that can confuse coders. Although, the text is Unicode, the representation is in binary data. It may seem laborious, at first, but it becomes easier as you get used to it. On the other hand, Python 2, uses a separate Unicode and an ASCH string.

4. "Look up" feature

In Python 3, the 'Look up' feature operates faster with integers than that of Python 2. If you're pressed for time, this is one major advantage that you can benefit from. This does not apply to floats, however.

Also, with regards to Python 3's range and Python 2's xrange for iterable objects that has to be run once, Python 3, typically, has the inclination to run slower. Nonetheless, for more than one, or for infinite iterations, Python 3 has the advantage.

5. New features

Python 3 has some new features that are not present in Python 2. If you're using Python 2, you have to import the features to your Python 2. This is done through the _future_ module.

These new Python 3 features include:

a. *'with' statement (with_statement)* – there will be times you will need this statement, so it's advantageous that Python 3 has provided it.

b. *Unicode literals (unicode_literals)* - this is one of the significant features for Python 3.

c. *2to3 utility* – the 2to3 utility regularly comes with the Python 3 interpreter. This is useful in converting Python 2 codes into functional Python 3 codes.

d. *Simple generators (generators)* – you can use these simple generators to create correct syntax for your Python codes. The process is simplified and quick.

e. *Raw_input function* – in Python 3, this function was rendered useless in a sense that the inputs are treated as strings.

f. *Statistically nested scopes (nested_scopes)* – at times you will have to create nested scopes, depending on your data.

g. *Create a print function (print_function)* – as discussed earlier, in Python 3, 'print' is now a function. So, when using the function, enclose your statements with parentheses. You may also want to create your own print function that you can use whenever necessary.

h. *Integer division* – Python 3 gives the answer to divisions, automatically, in a floating number form. Unlike Python 2, which has to round fractions into whole numbers, unless the numerator and denominator are expressed specifically as floating numbers. This makes math easier in Python 3.

i. *Exception arguments* – Python 3 exception arguments must be enclosed in parentheses to avoid SyntaxErrors, and should be stated with 'as'; while in Python 2, the parentheses may or may not be included. So, except is expressed as exc as var, instead of exc, var.

j. *Imports absolute relative and multi-line (absolute_import)* – this can be useful in preparing your codes. But it can become a problem if you have duplicate files.

k. *Changing the division operator (division)* – you can easily change your division operator.

If you're using Python 2, and you want to import these features you can use the command:

    future

Let's say you want to import unicode iterals, you can use this statement:

    >>>from_future_import unicode_literals

6. Iterable objects

Python 3 returns iterable objects, instead of lists, which Python 2 usually does. But, you can also convert the object to a list, whenever necessary. Using objects instead of list can save space in your device.

7. Rounding numbers

In rounding 0.5, Python 3 rounds off 0.5 by adding one to the preceding number - only - when the number can be rounded to an even number.

Examples for Python 3:

> *>>>round (20.5)*
> *20*
>
> *>>>round (21.5)*
> *22*
>
> *>>>round (13.5)*
> *14*

Examples for Python 2:

> *>>>round (20.5)*
> *21*
> *>>>round (21.5)*
> *22*
> *>>>round (13.5)*
> *14*

In Python 2, 0.5 will be rounded to 1 point, no matter what the type of number is obtained in the preceding number.

8. No returns in Python 3 for some functions

There are certain functions that no longer return a list. These are: the methods, such as .values ( ), .keys ( ) and .items ( ) from the dictionary; the map ( ), the filter ( ), and the zip( ).

9. Users' inputs

Python 3 has now the ability to store users' inputs as strings, thereby preventing error problems that had occurred in the earlier Python versions. This is convenient for fast-track coders, who want things to be done quickly but properly.

10.   'Next'( ) function

In Python 3, the next( ) function is used and not the .next() method, unlike Python 2. If you use the .next method in Python 3, an AttributeError results. This is one important fact that you must prioritize in your memory.

11. Syntactic changes

- In Python 3, use this:

  class C (metaclass=M):
  . . .

  instead of the old code:
  class C:
  ___metaclass___ = M

- In Python 3, ellipsis should now be spelled as .... (instead of ...), and can now be used anywhere, even outside the slices.
- Python 3 uses the list comprehension syntax, wherein the items are enclosed in parentheses.

Here's a table of syntaxes that were removed from Python 3

Removed/changed syntax	New Python 3 syntax
<>	!=
def foo (a, (b, c)) : ...	def foo (a, b_c) : b, c = b_c
raise_stmt: 'raise' [test [',' test [',' test]]]	raise_stmt: 'raise' [test]
exec() (removed as a keyword)	exec() remains as a function
backticks	repr
classic classes	
Trailing l or L (for	

integers)	
Leading u or U (for string literals)	

- Unpacking of tuple parameter is removed. This lessens some of the trivial procedures that you have to do with the old Python versions.

- For relative imports in Python 3, this code must be used:

  from. [module] import name

- Also, the code below is used only on the module level, and not on the inside functions:

  from module import*

12. There are slight changes in the modules' names too:

Name Changes

New Name	Old Name
configparser	ConfigParser
copyreg	copy_reg
_markupbase	markupbase
queue	Queue
reprlib	repr
socketserver	SocketServer
test.support	Test.test_support
Changes in the Library	
hashlib replaced gopherlib	
There are new modules for the Standard Library, such as: enum. (enumeration), statistics:, unittest.mock (for mock tests), pathlib (file system paths that are object-oriented) , asyncio (asynchronous IO), venv (virtual	

environment), faulthandler (debugging),

Take note that even a slight change in the lowercase and uppercase letters can spell a significant result. You can have return errors in the process. Therefore, be careful with your capitalizations.

13. In Python 3, numerous modules are improved and simplified. Some of these are: cmath, idlelib and IDLE, pprint, zipfile, code, pydoc, xml, poplib, math, pdb, logging, pickle, shelve, and many more.

The changes may seem enormous, but in the long run, as you prepare your codes, the builtin support systems will assist you.

There are still numerous small changes, as the Python 3 is updated to more advanced versions. Nonetheless, Python will always find a way to make users adjust easily through helpful modules, functions or methods.

Chapter 3: Most Common Python 3 Data Types

Python uses data extensively. There are various data types that are commonly used in the Python versions. The data types have not changed, but the manner they are treated in Python 3 have some differences.

Python 3 data types

1. ### <u>Numbers</u>

   As previously stated, Python 3 supports all types of numbers: floating, complex, integers, exponents, and fractions.

   Usually, floating point numbers are used for Python 3. Since numbers are immutable, they are used extensively in various ways, such as in indices, arithmetic, expressing positions, and in manipulating strings, lists and tuples.

   In the next chapter, you will learn how to make use of Python 3 as a powerful calculator.

2. ### <u>Strings</u>

   Strings are letters, numbers or symbols that are enclosed in, either, double quotes or single quotes. These enclosed characters can be constants or variables, such as numbers, texts and letters.

   In Python 3, the string must be enclosed in quotes, or a return error will occur.

   Example #1:

   > >>*"Hello, I'm Dave and this is my Python statement."*

   Example #2:

   > >>*"Python 3 is cool!"*

   Example #3:

> >>>*"I want to learn more about the Python language."*

You can print your strings, if you want to, just call on the 'print' function.

Example #1:

> >>>*print ("Hello, I'm Dave and this is my Python statement.")*

> *Hello, I'm Dave and this is my Python statement.*

Example #2:

> >>>*print ("Python 3 is cool!")*

> *'Python is cool.'* #output from interpreter.

Example #3:

> >>>*print ("I want to learn more about the Python language.")*

> *'I want to learn more about Python language.'* #output from interpreter

Reminder:

- Always enclose your strings with parentheses to identify that these are strings.

- Numbers can be converted to strings, if you want to use them as strings.

3. **<u>Tuples</u>**

Tuples are like strings. This is because they contain the same type of items as strings, only, these are enclosed by parentheses, instead of brackets. The values of the variables in tuples cannot be changed – just like the strings; they are immutable. On the other hand, the values of the variables in the lists can be changed; they are mutable.

Tuples can also be a combination of integers (numbers) or letters, which are generally, homogenous

Example #1:

>>>tuple1 = ('Leila', 'Well', 34, 'New York', 1021)

Example #2:

>>>tuple2 = (467, 'Lena')

Example #3:

>>>tup3 = (87, "New York", "Arts")

4. **Booleans**

These values represent two constant values – True or False. They determine if the value is true or not. The builtin function bool ( ) is used to convert non-Boolean values to Boolean values.

Example #1

>>>2<5
True

Example #2

>>>15==12
False

Example #3

>>>4*2 !=10
True

5. **Dictionaries**

These data come from builtin (built-in) or created dictionaries. The keys for dictionaries must not be changed. So, strings, tuples or numbers can be used as keys because these are all immutable.

Python 3 dictionaries will be discussed more in the upcoming chapter. The associated punctuation mark or symbol for dictionaries are the curly brackets.

6. **Lists**

When there are more than one string, they comprise a list. The values and variables of a list can be sliced, concatenated, or modified. It can contain various data types or the same data types.

Example #1:

>>>['cabbages', 'potatoes', 'eggplants', 'carrots']

Example #2:

>>>['pencil', 'paper', 'notebook, 'book']

If you want to name your lists, you can do so by assigning names that are related to their contents.

>>>myVeggies = ['cabbages', 'potatoes', 'eggplants', 'carrots']

>>>mySchoolMaterials = ['pencil', 'paper', 'notebook, 'book']

Or:

>>>list1 = ['cabbages', 'potatoes', 'eggplants', 'carrots']

>>>list2 = ['pencil', 'paper', 'notebook, 'book']

It's up to you to name your lists in a manner that would make you remember them easily. This is because you can use them later on just by 'calling' out their names.

You can then print these lists by calling out the 'print' function.

Example #1:

If you want to print my veggies, you can create your Python 3 statement this way:

>>>*print ['cabbages', 'potatoes', 'eggplants', 'carrots']*

'cabbages', 'potatoes', 'eggplants', 'carrots' #This is the returns of the interpreter

or

>>>*print [myVeggies]*

'cabbages', 'potatoes', 'eggplants', 'carrots' #you will be obtaining the same returns.

Example #2:

>>>*['pencil', 'paper', 'notebook, 'book']*

'pencil', 'paper', 'notebook', 'book'

7. **Sets**

These are data types composed of unorganized elements that have no duplicate values found in the same set.

The function keyword set() or set{} is used to create sets or empty sets. The curly brackets is also used in creating a dictionary, thus, the function keyword, set(), is preferable.

Python set objects support words, numbers, letters, names and anything that can be inputted into your data files.

Example #1:

>>>*set1 = {"eggplants", "carrots", "beans", "cabbage", "beans"}*
>>>*print (set1)*
{"eggplants", "carrots", "beans", "cabbage"}

Notice that "beans" has been duplicated, and was removed from the list. If you want to do it more quickly, you can apply the membership function.

Example #1:

>>>*"beans" in set1*

True

Example #2:

>>>"celery" in set1
False

Frozen sets

These are sets that are immutable. Typically sets are mutable although they contain immutable objects.

Example:

>>>subjects = frozenset (["geometry", "physics", "astronomy", "science"])

Operations for sets

clear() – this function will clear all elements of the set.

Example:

>>>subjects = {"geometry", "physics", "astronomy", "science"}

>>>subjects.clear()

set()

difference() – this method or function will return the difference between two or more sets. There are times you need to know the data from this method, especially with integers.

Example:

>>>a = {"a", "b", "c", "d", "e"}

>>>b = {"a", "b", "c"}

>>>a.difference(b)

{"d", "e"}

You can also do this:

>>>*a-b* #this will show the elements in set a that are not present in set b

You will obtain the same return/output.

{"d", "e"}

If you want to know the elements in either set a or set b, use: a|b. This will also return the unduplicated elements in either of the sets.

Example:

>>>*a|b*

{"a", "b", "c", "d", "e"}

If you want to access the elements found in both set a and set b, you can use: a & b.

Example:

>>>*a & b*

{"a", "b", "c"}

If you want to access unduplicated elements found in set a and set b, use:

a ^ b.

Example:

>>>*a ^ b*

{"d", "e"}

add(element)

This method adds an immutable element to a set.

Example:

>>>*Names = {"Dixon", "Johnson", "White"}*

>>>*names.add("Leonard"}*

>>>*names*

{"Leonard" "Dixon", "Johnson", "White"}

discard(element)

You can discard any element in the set by using the method or function discard(element). You can also use remove(element). A KeyError is returned if the specified element is not found.

Example:

>>>*a = {"a", "b", "c", "d", "e"}*

>>>*a.discard("b")*

>>>*a*

{"a", "c", "d", "e"}

All of these methods are useful in manipulating your data and organizing them into meaningful files.

You don't have to memorize all of them, you can always refer to these methods, when you want to use them.

Chapter 4: Using Python 3 as a Calculator

Similar to Python 2, you can also use Python 3 to compute or calculate math equations and to solve problems. Yes, Virginia, it's also a calculator!

You can add, subtract, divide or multiply using Python's interactive interpreter. The math operators are the common ones you use every day; therefore, you would not have any problem working with them.

Set up the calculator by clicking on the interpreter and then use the math symbols, just like you use them in your simple calculator.

When the three arrow signs appear >>>, you can start typing your numbers. When you press enter, the answer will appear in the next line.

Solving simple math problems

Examples:

>>>3 + 12

15

>>>56 – 13

43

>>>8*12

96

>>>36/3

12

Based on the example above, you can conclude the following meanings:

+ sign for addition

- sign for subtraction

/ sign for division

* sign for multiplication

For division, if you want to compute for the remainder, you can use the percent sign % (modulus).

If you want to round off an answer with fractions, you can use the sign //. This is because the sign / will always give an answer in a floating number form.

Floating numbers are numbers expressed with decimal points. Examples are: 4.5, 6.0, 3.10, and 8.0.

The other types of numbers are the integers (int) Examples are: 1, 2, 3, 4, and 5.

Solving for the square of numbers

To solve for the square of numbers, you can use the sign **.

Example:

4^3

>>>4**3

64

5^3

>>>5**3

125

The use of the equal sign =

The equal sign = is used when assigning values to variables. It's not used to show equality. Again, in Python 2 and 3, the = sign does not mean the values are equal. It indicates the values of the variable.

Examples:

>>>var mystring

>>>mystring = ("grapes", "bananas", "apples")

When values are not assigned to variables, the interpreter will return an error.

The double equal sign = = indicates equal values. This is the symbol of equality.

Examples:

>>>4 * 4 ==16

>>>5 * 10 == 50

>>>8*2 ==16

>>>6/3==2

You can use the name of the variable instead of the actual numbers.

Examples:

>>>myvariable1==5

>>>myvariable2==10 - 2

Instead of adding 5 + (10 -2), you can simply type:

>>>myvariable1 + myvariable2

Then press enter or run. The answer will appear in the next line. The answer will be 13.

13

You can prioritize what the Python 3 interpreter will solve first by using the parentheses.

Example:

>>>(3*8)+ (19-5) #3*8 will be solved first, then 19-5, before they are added

Thus, the answer will be:

>>>(3*8) + (19-5)

278

The # sign indicates that the succeeding statement is a comment and is not part of the equation.

In the absence of a parentheses, the computation will apply the common MDAS rule. The order in which the problem is solved is" multiplication, division, addition and then subtraction.

If parentheses are present, the numbers inside the parentheses are prioritized, and if there are number with exponents, they are next to be computed. Then the MDAS follow.

MDAS stands for Multiplication, Division, Addition and Subtraction.

When a part of the math equation is imaginary, instead of x, the letter j or J is assigned as a suffix.

Examples:

$10j + 240$

$9 + 2j$

Python 3 recognizes these types of numbers: integers, floating, fractions, decimals, and complex numbers.

When numbers are used as strings, they are not enclosed in quotes.

Comparison operations

These comparison operations are typically built-in into interpreters, so you can proceed in interpreting your data. The operators are straightforward like the symbols that you are familiar with:

1. **== indicates equality**

   Examples:

   ```
   3==3
   2*3==6
   4/2==2*1
   ```

2. **!= indicates non-equality**

   Examples:

   ```
   3!=4
   2*3!=8
   8/4!=6
   ```

3. **< indicates less than**

   Examples:

   8<12
   7<10

4. **> indicates more than**

   Examples:

   10>8
   4>5

5. **<= indicates less than or equal**

   Example:

   'a'<='b'
   'b'<='c'

6. **>= indicates greater than or equal**

   Example:

   'a'>='b'
   'b'>='c'

7. **is indicates object identity**

8. **is not indicates a negated object identity**

Take note that the objects compared should be of the same types for you to be able to compare them reliably.

Numeric operations

The numeric operations are prioritized more than the comparison operations. These operations are vital when using integers, complex numbers and floating point numbers to create specific numbers.

1. **x + y**

   This denotes the sum of x and y.

Example:

>>>x=4
>>>y=5
>>> x + y
9

2. **x − y**

This denotes the difference between x and y.

Example:
>>>x=10
>>>y=6
>>>x-y
4

3. **x * y**

This denotes the product of x and y.

Example:

>>>x =6
>>>y=3
>>>x*y
16

4. **x / y**

This denotes the quotient of x divided by y.

Example:

>>>x=12
>>>y=4
>>>x/y
3

5. **x // y**

This denotes the floored quotient of x and y.

Example #1:

```
>>>x=13
>>>y=4
>>>x//y
3
```

Example #2:

```
>>>x=15
>>>y=6
>>>x//y
2
```

6. x % y

This denotes the remainder, when x is divided by y.

Example #1:

```
>>>x=17
>>>y=5
>>>x % y
4
```

Example #2:

```
>>>x =12
>>>y = 5
>>>x % y
4
```

7. -x

This denotes that the x value is negated or was proven untrue.

8. +x

This denotes that the x value remained unchanged.

9. abs (x) or abs( )

This denotes the absolute value of x.

10.   int (x) or int( )

This denotes that x will be converted to an integer (number).

11. float (x) or float ( )

This denotes that x will be converted to a floating point number

12. complex(re, im) or complex( )

This denotes the real (re) and imaginary (im) values of a complex number.

13. c.conjugate()

This denotes the conjugate of c (complex number).

14. divmod (x, y) or divmod( )

This denotes the pair (x // y, x % y)

15. pow(x, y) or pow( )

This denotes that x is raised to the power y.

16. x**y

This is another method of expressing exponents. It's the same as #15, which is x to the power y.

Versions of Python 3 may have minor changes, but don't worry, you will be fully informed of future changes by Python's official website.

Chapter 5: Variables in Python 3

Variables are considered as storage locations of values. Variables are given specific names related to the values they contain. They act as labels for these values. Variables allow easy storage and retrieval of files from your computer or device, because all you have to do to access them, is to 'call' them out using their labels or names.

Steps for creating variables

Step #1 – Name your variable

The first thing that you must do is to name your variable in a manner that you could identify the values it contains without difficulty.

Example:

If you have a variable contain your grocery list, you may want to name it, 'groc', or 'groclist', or simply 'groceries'.

Step #2 – Use the assignment operator (equal sign =) to assign the values

You can now assign the values of your variable by using = , which is the assignment operator.

Example #1:

>>>var1 = ("Welcome")

>>>print ("Welcome')

Welcome

Example #2:

>>>myVar = 10

>>>print (myVar)

10

Example #3:

>>>myVar + 3

13

Example #4:

>>>*myVar * 5*

50

Example #5:

>>>*print (var1, "to my world")*

Welcome to my world

Step #3 – Use your variable

Now that you have assigned values to your variable, you can now use it. The name of the variable can be used in calculations, just by using the variable name, if the assigned value is an integer.

Example #1:

>>>*myVar = 10*

>>>*myVar – 5*

5

This means that you can use the name of the variable in any way you can. The value of your variables will be the value that will be considered in the Python statements.

But, before you use your variable in any statement, you have to define it first to assign its value/s.

Storing variables in other variables

You can store your variable in another variable by equating the second variable with the first variable.

Example:

>>>*var2 = 11*

>>>*var3 = var2*

>>>*print (var3)*

Hence, the value of var3 would also be 10, when run in Python.

Example: as shown above

>>>*print (var3)*

11

However, you can change the value of var2, and still allow var3 to be =11.

Local variables

These are variables that are defined inside a function. They have vital roles inside the function, but they are not related to variables outside of the function, even if they have the same names.

Example:

>>>*def func () :*

x=15

>>>x = 22

The first x is found inside the function - func, while the second x is found outside of the function.

The value of the x found inside the function will not affect that of the other x. Hence, if you call x, it will give the value 11.

Example:

>>>*print (x) or x*

22

>>>*func()*

15

But you can change the value of the x outside the function to a global value by using def function.

Example:

>>>def func() :

    global x

    x = 15

    print (x)

When you try to call the values of the x inside the function and the x outside of the function, you will have these returns:

Examples:

>>>func()

15

>>>x

15

Illegal names for variables

There are terms that you cannot use in naming your variables because they will return an error. They are called illegal names.

1. **Names starting with numbers** – the variable name must not be a number, or must not start with a number.

   Example:

   45myList
   10variable
   89cents

2. **Names starting with the dollar sign $** - Your variable names must NOT start with a dollar sign.
   Example:

$myList
$myVariables
$tuples

3. **Names using Python keywords** – Keywords are considered as illegal names, so don't use them. You will know that it's a keyword, when the color of the letters change to a different color. (i.e. black to brown), as you type it.

Example:

func_variable
printNames
defList1

4. **Spaces between words in the name** – There should be NO spaces between words in your variable names. If you have two words, you can use an underscore _ to denote that they are two words. You can also capitalize the first letter of the second word, similar to camelCase. The first letter of the first word is in the lowercase.

Examples:

employee_names or employeeNames

my_variable or myVariable

patients_id or patientsID

Reminders

- When you reassign a variable, the previous value will be deleted. So, if you don't intend to delete your previous variables, don't duplicate the variables' names.

- Never use similar variable names. Create unique names. This is to avoid messing up your files.

- Name your variables properly and you won't encounter any problems in the future.

Knowing how to properly name your variables may seem a trivial task but its effect is enormous. You can lose your important files just because of your carelessness. Don't let that happen to you. Learn how to do the procedure correctly.

Chapter 6: Manipulating Strings

Strings were defined in the previous chapter. This chapter will deal with the process of manipulating or modifying your strings. Strings are enclosed in single or double quotes, and they are immutable.

More examples of strings:

Example #1:

>>>("What did you learn from the previous chapters?")

'What did you learn from the previous chapters?'   #This is the output
after   press enter.

Example #2:

>>>('I hope you enjoy learning Python.')

'I hope you enjoy learning Python.'

You can easily manipulate your strings using Python 3. I will present this chapter in simple terms. Hopefully, it will help you understand the concept.

<u>Here are vital facts that you must remember.</u>

Escaping quotes

You can escape quotes by using the backslash sign \

Example #1:

>>>print ("I don/'t want to go there.")

'I don't want to go there.'

Example #2:

>>>print ('He doesn\'t want to go there.')

"He doesn't want to go there.'

You can also use triple quotes when strings are too long.

Example:

>>>"""*This doesn/'t make sense to me," he said."""*

'This doesn't make sense to me', he said.

Concatenating strings

You can quickly concatenate (add) strings by making use of the plus sign + . You can also repeat the concatenation by using the asterisk symbol * .

Example #1:

>>>*str1 = "Pac"*

'Pac'

>>>*str2 = "man"*

'man'

>>>*str1 + str2*

'Pacman'

Example #2:

>>>*"hydrogen" + "peroxide"*

'hydrogen peroxide'

Example #3:

>>>*2 * "hydrogen" + "peroxide"* #2 * indicates that the string must be repeated twice (2x)

'hydrogen hydrogen peroxide'

Two string literals that are beside each other are usually concatenated automatically.

Example #1:

>>>*"Justice" "prevails"*

'Justice prevails'

Example #2:

>>>*"Python" "language"*

'Python language'

Creating new strings

You can create new strings from old strings or new data. You cannot change your strings but you can do various procedures with them.

Example #1: Let's use the previous examples

>>>*"Super" + str2*

'Superman'

Take note that the results (without the arrow prompts) will only appear when you press 'enter', 'execute' or 'run' the command.

Ensure that you're referring to the correct string name. In Python 3, the first letter of the first word of the variables are usually in small letters, then the first letter of the second word, or the third word may be in the uppercase.

Indexing strings

You can assign indices to strings starting from 0 and onwards. You can also do the reverse indexing, where values start at -1, for the second character from the last.

Take note that each string is enclosed in single or double quotes.

Example #1:

If the string is "computer", the table below will show you how the indexes are assigned:

str1 = "computer'

Values in the string	c	o	m	p	u	t	e	r
Assigned (+) indexes	0	1	2	3	4	5	6	7
Assigned (-) indexes	-7	-6	-5	-4	-3	-2	-1	

Example #2:

str2 = "This is my Python 3 world."

Values in the string	This	is	my	Python	3	world
Assigned (+) indexes	0	1	2	3	4	5
Assigned (-) indexes	-5	-4	-3	-2	-1	

If you are to slice the string, you can simply refer to their indexes using square brackets [ ]. If you want to indicate the start and end of your slice, use [:]. This will be discussed more in the topic, slicing strings.

Slicing strings

You can slice your strings and create new strings. As stated earlier, strings are immutable, so they cannot be changed. However, you can create new strings from the old strings, or from new data.

Example #1:

>>>str1 = 'computer'

'computer'

>>>str1[2]

'm'

Example #2:

>>>str1 = 'computer'

'computer'

>>>str1[3]

'p'

Example #3:

>>>str1 = 'computer'

'computer'

>>>str1[1:3] #This means that the starting index you want the interpreter to return is index 1 up to index 2.

Hence, when you press enter, the results will be:

'om'

If you want to include up to letter 'p', your Python 3 code should be:

>>>str1[1:4].

If you enter a non-existent index, the Python 3 interpreter will return an error.

Example:

>>>str1[8]

TypeError: 'str' object does not support item assignment.

Example #1 Let's use the string for the above example #2.

>>>str2 = "This is my Python 3 world."

'This is my Python 3 world.'

>>>str2 [2]

'is'

Example #2:

>>>str2[2:4]

'my Python'

Example #3:

>>>str2[2:5]

'my Python 3'

If you want to display an index starting from a certain index up to the last one, you can create your Python syntax/code this way:

Example #1:

>>>str1[1:]

'omputer'

Example #2:

>>>str2[1:]

'is my Python 3 world.'

If you want to obtain the first indexed value up to a certain index, you can create your Python statement this way:

Example #1:

>>>str1[:5]

'compu'

Example #2:

>>>str2[:5]

'This is my Python 3'

Example #3:

>>>str2[:6]

'This is my Python 3 world.'

Determining the length of the string

You can quickly determine the length of the string by using the function key, len(). This step is important if you intend to modify your indexes.

Example #1:

>>>*len (str1)*

7

Example #2:

>>>*len(str2)*

5

Example #3:

>>>*myName = "LeilaFaulker"*

'LeilaFaulker'

>>>*len(myName)*

11

In the examples, you can observe that the length of str1[2:5] is 3.

Updating strings

Strings can be updated by assigning the variable you want to be updated to another string.

Example:

>>>*var = "Love makes the world go round!"*

>>>*print ("Updated String : ", var[0:] + "Hope")*

"Hope makes the world go round!"

Special operators for strings

+ *Concatenation (adding).* You can use this operator to add your strings.

[] *Slice,* the index is indicated inside the square brackets. This index

represents the character in the string.

[:] *Range-slice,* the range of the indices is given. These indices represent

the characters in the string.

* This denotes repetition of the string. As you know now, strings are immutable, so you will

Be creating new strings.

% *Format,* it indicates that strings are being formatted.

in Membership, this returns a True value, if the specified item is found in the string.

Example #1:

>>>myString = *"Love makes the world go round!"*

>>>*the in (myString)*

True

Example #2:

>>>myString = *"Love makes the world go round!"*

>>>*hope in (myString)*

False

not in It's the opposite of in. This returns a True value, if the specified item or character is not found in the string.

Example:

>>>*hope not in (myString)*

True

Chapter 7: Modifying Python 3 Lists

Python 3 (i.e. Python 3.5.2, 3.5.1, 3.1) lists are mutable; therefore, they can be changed or modified. Lists have been defined in the previous chapter as a group of data – usually homogenous – that comprise a list.

The items in the list is similar to the items in a string. They can be any of the various types of data. Each item in the lists is separated by a comma. The lists use brackets to enclose all the values they contain.

Example #1:

>>>names = ["Jones", "Clinton", "Stewart", "Woods"]

Example #2:

>>>numbers = [210, 110, 305, 310]

Example #3:

>>>myList = ["Geometry", "average", "passed"]

Indexing lists

You can index lists just like you can index strings. The indexing starts at 0, and then so forth. You can also apply reverse indexing starting with -1 - from the second item from the end of the list.

Example #1:

>>>names = ["Jones", "Clinton", "Stewart", "Woods"]

Example #2:

>>>numbers = [210, 110, 305, 310]

Example #3:

>>>myList = ["Geometry", "average", "passed"]

When you press 'enter', 'run' or 'execute' after you have inputted examples #1, #2 and #3, after the arrow prompt >>>, the returns/results or return data will be the next line after the Python statements (statements after the prompt >>>).

See examples below:

Example #1:

>>>names = ["Jones", "Clinton", "Stewart", "Woods"]

>>>print (names)

['Jones', 'Clinton', 'Stewart', 'Woods']

Example #2:

>>>numbers = [210, 110, 305, 310]

[210, 110, 305, 310]

Example #3:

>>>myList = ["Geometry", "average", "passed"]

>>>print (myList)

['Geometry', 'average', 'passed']

Methods for list objects

Clearing a list

List.clear ()- you can clear the items in the list by using the method key, list.clear(). This is the same as del a[:]

Example:

>>>list.clear(myList)

Or

>>>del myList[:]

All of the items in the list, "Geometry", "average", "passed", will be deleted.

Appending a list

List.append() – you can append an item to the end of your list by using the method key, list.append( ). The new item is positioned at the last.

Example #1:

>>>names = ["Jones", "Clinton", "Stewart", "Woods"]

["Jones", "Clinton", "Stewart", "Woods"]

>>>names.append("Lewis")

>>>print (names)

['Jones', 'Clinton', 'Stewart', 'Woods', 'Lewis']

Example #2:

>>>numbers = [210, 110, 305, 310]

[210, 110, 305, 310] #return or output

>>>numbers.append(330)

[210, 110, 305, 310, 330] #return or output

Example #3:

>>>myList = ["Geometry", "average", "passed"]

['Geometry', 'average', 'passed']

>>>myList.append("incomplete")

print (myList)

['Geometry', 'average', 'passed', 'incomplete']

Example #4:

>>>list = [2, 4, 6, 8 10]

>>>list.append(12)

>>>print list

[2, 4, 6, 8 10, 12] #return or output

Inserting an item in a list

List.insert() – you can insert an item into your list by using the method key list.insert( ). This command is similar to a.insert(i, x), where i is the index number, where you want the x (item) to be inserted.

Example #1:

>>>myList = ["Geometry", "average", "passed"]

>>>myList.insert(0, "Thomas") #This means that at index 0, "Thomas" will be inserted.

>>>print (myList)

['Thomas', 'Geometry', 'average', 'passed'] #return or output

Example #2:

>>>myList = ["Thomas", "Geometry", "average", "passed"]

['Geometry', 'average', 'passed']

>>>myList.insert(1, "Daniels")

print (myList)

['Thomas', 'Daniels', 'Geometry', 'average', 'passed']

The difference between list.append( ) and list.insert( ), is that in the former, the item you want to append (add) is appended at the end of the list. Meanwhile, in list.insert( ), you can select the index of your inserted item. For most coders, the latter is preferable.

Counting the number of times an item appears in a list

List.count(x) – list.count(x). You can easily count the number of times x is found in the specified list. This is a good data to identify duplicates too.

Example #1:

>>>names = ["Jones", "Clinton", "Stewart", "Woods"]

>>>list.count("Woods")

>>>print (value)

1

Example #2:

>>> *grades = [85, 88, 92, 88, 97]*

>>>*grades.count(88)*

2

List.count(x) is typically used when there are existing loops.

Copying a list

This is used when you want a copy of the list. It's the same as a[:]. The method's key is list.copy( ).

Example #1:

>>> *grades = [85, 88, 92, 88, 97]*

>>>*finalGrades = grades [:]*

[85, 88, 92, 88, 97]

Or

>>> *grades = [85, 88, 92, 88, 97]*

>>>*grades.copy()*

[85, 88, 92, 88, 97]

Sorting a list

sorted()

You can sort the items in a list by simply calling the function sorted(). This will sort iterable items, as well.

Example #1:

>>>*grades = [85, 88, 92, 88, 97]*

[85, 88, 92, 88, 97]

>>> *sorted ([85, 88, 92, 88, 97])*

[85, 88, 88, 92, 97]

It has been sorted in an ascending order, from lowest to highest.

List.sort()

You can also use the method key, list.sort(). This is useful when you need the original list.

Example:

>>> *grades = [85, 88, 92, 88, 97]*

[85, 88, 92, 88, 97]

>>> *list.sort ([85, 88, 92, 88, 97])*

>>> *grades*

[85, 88, 88, 92, 97]

list.reverse()

You could also reverse the list with the command, list.reverse(). This will present the list in a reverse manner.

Example:

>>> *grades = [85, 88, 92, 88, 97]*

>>>*grades.reverse ()*

>>>*print (grades)*

[97, 92, 88, 88, 85]

Extending a list
list.extend(L)

You can extend or concatenate (add) one list to another. If you have numerous relate data, you can organize the and combine them to save space.

Example #1:

>>>*studentNames = ["Osmond", "Trump", "Delano", "Lauren"]*

>>>*studentSections =["a", "b", "c", "d"]*

>>>*studentNames.extend(studentGrades)*

>>>print studentNames

['Osmond', 'Trump', 'Delano', 'Lauren', 'a', 'b', 'c', 'd']

Removing items from a list

list.remove(x) – this is used to remove a value from the list that is first and has the specified value of that you're looking for. Naturally, a delete (del) statement can be used too to remove the element or value from the list; similar to slicing strings.

Example #1:

>>>studentNames = ["Osmond", "Trump", "Delano", "Lauren"]

>>>studentNames.remove("Trump")

>>>print (studentNames)

['Osmond', 'Delano', 'Lauren']

You can also use the keyword, del, to delete items in a list. You can delete all, except the last item.

Example #2: (Using the same data above)

>>>del studentNames [:1]

>>>print studentNames

['Lauren']

You can also delete all, except the first element. You only have to indicate this inside the square brackets.

Example #2:

>>>>>>del studentNames [1:]

>>>print studentNames

['Osmond']

Example #3: (delete all except last 3 elements)

>>>del studentNames [:3]

>>>print studentNames

['Trump', 'Delano', 'Lauren']

Reminders:

- Again, the lines with the prompts, `>>>`, are the Python statements, while the lines without the prompts `>>>`, are the output or result after pressing 'enter', 'run' or' execute'. Thus, even without the hash (#) stating it's an output, if the statement has no arrow-prompt, you have to know that it's either an output or a comment.

  I hope you will remember this as you read the given examples.

Chapter 8: Using Lists as Queues and Stacks

There are various things you can do to your list. This is one of its advantages as a data type. Aside from being mutable, you can modify or manipulate it to serve your purpose; two of them is using lists as queues or stacks.

Lists as queues

Lists can also be used as queues. The elements in the list are 'queued' (in line) for the addition of a new element, either at the start, or at the end of the list.

The keyword for this is collection.deque.

Example:

> >>>*from collections import deque*
>
> >>>*namesqueue = ["Lovely", "Vincent", "Dean", "Landon"]*
>
> >>>*namesqueue = deque (["Lovely", "Vincent", "Dean", "Landon"])*
>
> >>>*namesqueue.append("James")*

In queues, usually, the first to 'arrive' is the first to 'go'. In the example above, "Lovely" was the first to arrive, therefore she goes first in the queue, and then so on.

Using the list.popleft() or queue.popleft() command, you can remove elements that you don't need in your list.

If you dequeu the namesqueue, using popleft(), the result will be:

> >>>*namesqueue.popleft()*
>
> *deque (['Vincent", "Dean", "Landon", James'])*

Lists as stacks

Lists can be used as stacks, as well. It's the opposite of queues, in the sense that the last element in, will be the first element out.

The command key in retrieving elements at the top of the stack is pop().

Example #1:

>>>*myStack = [1, 2, 3, 4, 5]*

>>>*myStack.append(6)*

>>>*print (myStack)*

[1, 2, 3, 4, 5, 6]

>>>*myStack.pop()*

6

>>>*print (myStack)*

[1, 2, 3, 4, 5]

Reminders:

Keep in mind that many of the rules in data modification are similar with strings and lists. If you know the rules for strings, then, more or less, you have an idea of the rules applicable for lists too.

List comprehension

List comprehension will help you create lists with relative ease, especially new lists coming from other operations. This is a Python feature that is of great help to coders.

Example:

>>>*celsius [3, 6, 9, 11, 13, 15]*

>>>*for x in range [6] :*

       *celsius.append (x**2)*

>>>*celsius*

[9, 36, 81, 121, 169, 225]

This example is just to show you how it works.

Parts of list comprehension

Learning about the parts of list comprehension will be helpful in your Python coding. These are:

1. **Sequence set** - this is where values are inputted.
2. **Variable** – this will specify the items of the inputs.
3. **Predicate** – this is an expression that you may or may not include.
4. **Output** – this will be the result of the #3 process, which will respond to the input's needed process.

More examples:

Example #2:

>>>grams = [10, 5.2, 8, 30]

>>>milligrams = [((float(1000)*x) for x in grams]

>>>print(mmilligrams)

[10000, 520, 8000, 30000]

You may want to practice creating your codes on your own with your IDLE interpreter. Discover how a few tweaks can produce different results. Enjoy!

Chapter 9: Tuples Definition and Purposes

Tuples are Python sequence data types that are immutable (unchangeable). They are like strings and numbers. But, it's important to note that they can contain mutable objects. The tuple contains Python objects or various values that can be heterogenous – meaning they can be data of different types.

Similar to strings and lists, the items/elements/values in tuples are separated by commas. Tuples are enclosed in parentheses, while lists are enclosed in square brackets.

Purposes of tuples

Contains heterogenous data - unlike lists, tuples generally contain heterogenous data that can be organized properly.

Example #1:

>>>myTuple = ("Smallville", 2010, 3456)

>>>print (myTuple)

('Smallville', 2010, 3456)

Example #2:

>>>tup1 = (2478, 1810, "Midtown St. Arizona")

>>>print (tup1)

(2478, 1810, 'Midtown St. Arizona')

Example #3: (nested tuples)

>>>tup2 = ((2478, 1810, "Midtown St. Arizona"), (910, 234, "Lafayette St. Arizona"))

Updating tuples

You can update tuples by creating new tuples from the values of existing tuples. Again, this is due to the fact that they are immutable or unchangeable.

Example:

>>>id = (1021, 1022, 1023, 1024)

>>>surnames = ("Walters", "Bell", "Getty", "Dalton")

>>>employees = id + surnames

>>>print (employees)

(1021, 1022, 1023, 1024, 'Walters', 'Bell', 'Getty', 'Dalton') #output

Slicing indexes of tuples

You can access values of indices or indexes by slicing the tuples using the square brackets [ ]. In some way, the process is similar to slicing strings. You identify the index and specify inside the brackets what you want to slice.

Example #1:

>>>tup1 = ("Romeo", "Grey", "Zainne")

If you want to slice or access "Grey" only from tup1, you can create your Python 3 syntax this way:

>>>print ("tup1[1] : ", tup1[1])

tup1[1] = Grey

Example #2:

>>>tup2 = (1, 2, 3, 4, 5, 6, 7, 8, 9)

If you want to access/slice only indexes 2 to 6, you can create your code this way:

>>>print ("tup1[2:7] : ", tup1[2:7])

tup2[2:7]: [2, 3, 4, 5, 6]

Most common built-in tuple functions

len(tuple) – this function returns the length of the tuple, or the number of elements in the tuple.

Example:

>>>tup1 = ("Romeo", "Grey", "Zainne")

>>>print (len(tup1))

3

max(tuple) – this function returns the element in the tuple with the maximum or highest value.

Example:

>>>tup1, tup2 = ("Romeo", "Grey", "Zainne"), (367, 650, 310)

>>>print ("Max value element : ", max(tup1))

>>>print ("Max value element : ", max(tup2))

Max value element : Zainne #for tup1

Max value element : 650 #for tup2

min(tuple) – this function is the opposite of max(tuple). It returns the minimum value of the elements in the tuple.

Example #1:

>>>tup1 = ("engineering", "sciences", "accounting", "education")

>>>print ("min value element : ", min(tup1))

min value element : accounting

Example #2:

>>>tup2 = (20, 35, 10, 15, 45)

>>>print ("min value element : ", min(tup2))

min value element : 10

cmp(tuple1, tuple2) – this function is used in comparing the elements of two tuples.

Example:

>>>*tup1 = (1956, "Indiana")*

>>>*tup2 = (2010, "New York")*

>>>*print cmp(tup1, tup2)*

>>>*print cmp(tup2, tup1)*

When you press the 'enter', 'run', or 'execute' keys, the returns (output) will be:

1

-1

tuple(seq) – this built-in function converts a list into a tuple. But take note that lists are mutable and tuples are immutable.

Example:

>>>*myList = ["toothbrush", "toothpaste", "mouthwash", "mouthwash"]*

>>>*tuple1 = tuple(myList)*

>>>*print ("tuple elements : ", tuple1)*

tuple elements : ("toothbrush", "toothpaste", "mouthwash", "mouthwash")

Most common basic tuple operations

The manipulation of tuples is much the same way as manipulating your strings. But for clarity' sake, I will summarize them for you. As education experts say: "Repetition and application promotes better retention", so here goes:

Concatenation

Uses the plus sign + to indicate that you intend to add tuples. You can also call this updating your tuples.

Yes, it's similar to the process that applies to strings but this time, tuples are involved. It's all about adding existing tuples to create a new tuple.

Example:

>>>*tuple1 = (1920, "Madrid", "Velasco")*

>>>*tuple2 = (2016, "England", "Burbanks")*

>>>*tuple3 = (tuple1 + tuple2)*

>>>*print (tuple3)*

(1920, "Madrid", "Velasco", 2016, "England", "Burbanks") #output or results

Membership

Uses 'in' or 'not in' to determine if value is found or not found in the elements of the specified tuples.

Example:

>>>*5 in (4, 5, 6)*

True

Repetition

Uses asterisk * to repeat an element or a tuple.

Example #1:

>>>*print ("Love is the answer.", 345) * 5*

("Love is the answer.", 345, "Love is the answer.", 345, "Love is the answer.", 345, "Love is the answer.", 345, "Love is the answer.", 345)

Example #2:

>>>*print("Jonathan", 240, "Washington DC")*2*

("Jonathan", 240, "Washington DC", "Jonathan", 240, "Washington DC")

Length

Uses len(tuple) to determine the length of the characters or elements in a tuple. Please refer to the example above about builtin functions.

Iteration

Iterates an element or elements contained in a tuple. You can refer to the chapter on strings to learn more about how the process works.

Example:

>>>*for x in (4, 5, 6) : print (x, end= " ")*

4 5 6

Reminders:

The prompts will indicate that you have to input your Python statement. Before returns or outputs can appear.

Again, the statements without arrow-prompts are the returns or outputs, and after the Python code or statements, remember to press 'enter', 'run' or 'execute' to obtain returns.

Chapter 10: File Management

File management is crucial in Python 3 programming. Proper organization of your files will allow faster accomplishment of your computer language programming tasks, such as storing, retrieving and manipulating your text files.

Python 3 is compatible with most operating systems, such as Windows 10, centOS 7, Mac OS X, and Ubuntu 16.04. Python can also accommodate various file formats, such as txt, HTML, CSV, JavaScript and JSON.

But before you can learn managing your Python files, here are some basic codes that you should learn:

Basic codes

"w" = writing

"r" = reading

"x" = creating and writing to a new file

"r+" = reading and writing to the same file

"a" = appending to a file

Reading a file

When reading a file, all you have to do is open or access it with open() function, which is the default command.

>>>*open()*

>>>*open (filename, mode)*

Example:

fobj = open("filename.txt", "r")

You can also omit the "r" (read).

fobj = open("filename.txt")

or:

filename.read()

filename.readline() #Allows you to read the file per line

filename.readlines() #allows you to read the lines in the txt file.

Closing files

To close the file, all you have to do is use the file object method close (fobj).

Example:

fobj.close( )

The complete syntax is:

fobj =open("filename.txt")

for line in fobj:

print (line.rstrip ())

fobj.close()

After running this code, the file will open and you can read to your heart's content. If the file is short (example a quote), you can use this code instead.

>>>quote = open("filename.txt").readlines()

>>>print (quote)

Or

>>>quote = open ("filename.txt").read()

>>>print (quote[:])

Writing into a file

66

You can easily write into a file too. All you have to do is to use the method write( ), which is of the file handle object.

Example:

> *fh. ("filename.txt", "w")*
>
> *fh.write ("Live and let live.")*
>
> *fh.close( )*

Creating a file

If you want to create a txt file, you can do this by opening the text editor. Remember to name the file properly, so you can access it without difficulties later on.

Let's say you wanted to create a txt file for your research topics, and named it researchtopicsdm.txt

After you have opened the file and named it, you can now add content to your file.

Example: *researchtopicsdm.txt*

> *Diagnosis of Diabetes Mellitus (DM)*
>
> *Symptoms of DM*
>
> *Laboratory Tests*
>
> *Treatment of DM*
>
> *Effects of Insulin*
>
> *Prognosis of DM*

After you're done adding content, remember to save your file in your computer where you can retrieve it quickly using Python 3.

Next, you can now open the file in Python using the methods discussed above. Remember to open first a path for the file in Python with the code:

> *>>>researchtopicsdm_file = open (path, "r")*

You must also create a title variable ("Research Topics DM") in Python for the file, and store it as a string.

Example:

>>>*title = "Research Topics DM/n"*

Hence:

>>>*path = '/users/usersname/researchtopicsdm.txt'*

>>>*researchtopicsdm_file = open (path, "r")*

>>>*Research = researchtopicsdm_file.read()*

Since the variables for title and Research Topics for DM were created, you can now proceed to create your new file. Be careful though in naming your new file because if a previous file has the same name, it could be deleted if you fail to remedy the problem.

Hence, the new path would be:

>>>*path = '/users/usersname/new_researchtopicsdm.txt'*

Then, you can open your new file using the function, open(), with the 'w' mode. The 'w' mode is important to signify that you are intending to write and not to read only.

Example:

>>>*new_path = '/users/usersname/new_research.txt'*

>>>*new_research = open(new_path, "w")*

Next, you can start writing to your new file by using the file operation, <file>.write() with the new file consisting of a single parameter of a string.

You may want to use Python's print function, print(), too, so you can view your file.

Example:

> *>>>new_researchtopicsdm.write("Research Topics DM")*

> *>>>print (title)*

And

> *>>> new_researchtopicsdm.write(research)*

> *>>>print(research)*

Don't forget to close your files after working on them, using the codes:

> *>>>researchtopicsdm_file.close()*

> *>>>new_ research.close()*

As previously mentioned, you may lose your old similarly named file, if you don't.

Example of your complete code, which will appear this way:

> *>>>path = '/users/usersname/researchtopicsdm.txt'*

> *>>>researchtopicsdm_file = open (path, "r")*

> *>>>new_path = '/users/usersname/new_research.txt'*

> *>>>new_research = open(new_path, "w")*

> *>>>Title − "Research Topics on DM"*

> *>>> new_researchtopicsdm.write("Research Topics DM")*

> *>>>print (title)*

> *>>> new_researchtopicsdm.write(research)*

> *>>>print(research)*

>>>*researchtopicsdm_file.close()*

>>>*new_ research.close()*

You can double check if your new file, researchtopicsdm.txt', has been created in Python, by accessing it.

If it shows, then you have successfully created a new file.

Pickle module

The pickle module is used in converting Python object hierarchies into byte streams. You can employ pickling and unpickling (serialization and flattening) of data or object structures, when you want to use the data resulting from it.

- **Dump method**

    This method is used in dumping objects with the command:

    >>>*pickle.dump(obj, file [,protocol, *, fix_imports =True])*

Note:

You can reread dumped objects by using the method:

   pickle.load(file). pickle.load

Example:

   >>>*import pickle*

   >>>*religions = ["Confucianism", "Islam", "Christianity", "Buddhism"]*

   >>>*fh = open("data.pk1", "bw")*

   >>>*pickle.dump(religions, fh)*

   >>>*fh.close()*

Note:

   fh = file handle object

Reminder:

- A file has to be opened first before you can read or write.

Shelve module

The shelve module is a dictionary-like object that uses strings as keys to resolve the issues of the pickle module. The pickle module can only pickle one object at a time and this problem is done away with the shelve module.

It's relatively easy to use the shelve module. All you have to do is to import it and open it, and you can proceed smoothly with your commands.

Example:

> *>>>import shelve*

> *>>>s = shelve.open("name of shelve")*

There will be a return error if the file is not a shelve file, but shelve will allow you to create a new file.

After using the file, remember to close it with the command:

> *>>>s.close()*

Example:

> *>>>import shelve*

> *>>>doct = shelve.open("MyEnlightenment")*

> *>>>doct ["Revelation"] = {"book":"Revelation", "author":"John", "year":"8196"}*

> *>>>doct ["Romans"] = {"book":"Romans", "author":"Paul", "year":"5556"}*

> *>>>doct ["Corinthians"] = {"book":"Corinthians", "author":"Paul", "year":"5354"}*

The file could go on and on. Now, if you want to extract a value from the "MyEnlightenment" shelve, you can promptly do that by importing the shelve, opening the file and extracting the information. If you want to retrieve the information about the author of "Romans", here's how you can do it.

Example:

>>>*import shelve*

>>>*doct = shelve.open("MyEnlightenment")*

>>>*doct ["Romans"] ["author"]*

'Paul' #This is the output.

Reading and writing binary data

When reading and writing binary data you can use the open() function with the rb (read binary), or wb (write binary) mode. An example of binary data are those files used by sounds and images.

These binary sequence types include bytes, bytearray and memoryview. The byte and bytearray are maintained by memoryview.

Bytes – are interpreted as binary data that can only be applicable with ASCII. They are types of object that are immutable with values ranging from 0-255 (8-bits) stored.

Retrieval of the values is similar to obtaining the values of indexes from an array. Also, they share some similarities with strings literals. Likewise, with the construction of the Python statements. The only difference is the addition of the prefix b to the bytes literals. Single, double and triple quotes, or triple quoted quotes, (' ' ' or " " "), with matching end quotes, can be used.

Bytes can come in the form of literals, iterable of integers, zero-filled bytes objects or the binary data from the buffer protocol.

Example:

>>>*bytes ([30, 30, 30])*

Bytearrays – on the other hand contain mutable objects.

Struct module

The struct module interprets bytes as binary data and uses these, together with bytearrays, to implement the Buffer Protocol.

The Buffer Protocol is usually wrapped by a large memory buffer, and is used for special purposes that include analysis of integers or math expressions and image processing.

It has two sides, the buffer interface on the side of the producer, and the consumer's side.

The struct module is composed of various functions and exceptions. Here are some of them:

1. **struct.calcsize(fmt)** – returns size of struct

2. **struct.unpack_from(fmt, buffer, offset=0)** – indicates that unpacking from buffer will start from offset. This will be based on the fmt (format string).

3. **struct.unpack** – indicates the unpacking of the buffer from buffer.

4. **struct.error** – returns description of exception errors.

5. **struct.pack_into(fmt, buffer, offset, v1,v2,...)** – offset indicates the position, fmt – indicates the format, buffer is where bytes are written and v1 and v2 are the packed values.

6. **struct.iter_unpack(fmt, buffer)** – unpack this using string fmt, from the buffer buffer.

There are still several things that you could learn from unpacking. However, they are a little bit complex, so let's stop here.

Chapter 11: Debugging and Profiling

Learning how to profile and debug your codes is a skill that would be useful to you as a Python language programmer. The debugger and profiler are vital parts of your Python standard library.

Debuggers

A debugger allows you to go through your codes to analyze them and set certain breakpoints. It will help you in evaluating what's wrong with your code. It's also useful in providing source code listing.

(pdb)

This is the prompt used in calling for your debugger module.

Example:

> >>>*import pdb; pdb.set_trace()*

Most common debugger commands

1. **help [command]** – this can be used in critical instances when you need help. The 'help exec' will help you obtain help from the command function, and the 'help pdb' will display the full pdb module's documentation.

2. **tbreak [([filename:] lineno | function) [, condition]]** – this sets the temporary breakpoint. They are assigned reference numbers that you can use and refer to whenever necessary.

3. **break lineno | function) [, condition]], or break [([filename:] lineno | function) [, condition]]** – this set breakpoints in the current file or where it is specified.

4. **disable [bpnumber [bpnumber . . .]]** – this can disable breakpoints, but they can be enabled anew with a proper step.

5. **enable [bpnumber [bpnumber . . .]]** – this can enable breakpoints in your codes.

6. **clear [filename: lineno | bpnumber [bpnumber . . .]]** – this clears all breakpoints. But a confirmation is asked first. This is done without the arguments.

7. **up [count]** – this indicates that you should move the frame's level in the stack trace down. This will depend on the count specified.

8. **down[count]** – this indicates that you should move the frame's level in the stack trace down. This will depend on the count specified.

9. **bpnumber [condition]** – you can set a condition for the breakpoint. This condition should be true for the breakpoint to proceed.

10. **where** – the current frame can be indicated by an arrow. You can print the stack trace, accordingly.

Profilers

Profilers are modules used in benchmarking the Python code against the C code. This is done through the cProfile and the profile. The data or statistics provided by the profilers are called profiles. These are data on the program's length and frequency of execution.

You utilize the timeit module, as well. It deals with specific portions of your Python statements that you want to diagnose. The most commonly used profiler is the cProfile. Because of its usefulness in long-running programs, it's preferred by some language programmers.

Example #1:

>>>*import cProfile*

>>>*import re*

Example #2:

>>>*import cProfile*

>>>*import hashlib*

>>>*cProfile.run ("hashlib.md5('abcdefghijkl').digest()")*

6 function calls in 1.500 CPU per seconds

When you press execute, the results will show the return statements or the output. The results from this code will help you evaluate the speed of your code.

This will allow you to access cProfile and use its functionality. There are also functions provided by cProfile and profile modules. These are:

1. **profile.run(command, filename=None, sort= -1)**

   This is passed on to the exec(). The diagram below shows the flowchart of the process:

   profile.run

   exec()
   if no file name is found)

   stats (controls sorting of data)

2. **profile.runctx(commands, globals, locals, filename=None)**
   Operates similarly to profile.run, but it provides the command strings' global and local dictionaries.

Stats Class

This is used to analyze the profile obtained by the profiler.

>>>*class.pstats.Stats(*filenames or profile, stream=sys.stdout)*

This will provide an overview of all the statistics of the processes for evaluation. To be able to do this, it uses methods, such as add(*filenames) – additional information; strip.dirs() – modifies the object by stripping some portion; dump_stats(filename) – object is save in filename; sort_stats(*keys) – stats objects are sorted according to specifications; and the different print commands.

These objects are still undergoing evolution, so be on the lookout for the latest developments.

Chapter 12: The Significance of Python Dictionaries

Python dictionaries are crucial in creating and executing proper syntax and statements.

Learning the vital role of the built-in dictionary of Python will help you vastly in creating your codes.

Since you are beginner, I will try to simplify the complex terms to let you understand better, so you could apply your knowledge effectively.

Python 3 has some differences from Python 2, but you can easily learn them by understanding the idea. Let's start with the simple terms in the Python dictionary.

Maps

Python 3 dictionaries have maps (similar to lists). You can only access the values of these maps, if you use the correct and unique key for each map. Imagine that the map is a padlock that you could only open with one specific key found within one dictionary.

The keys can be immutable data types, such as strings and numbers. You can imagine maps as key:value pairs that you can store and extract later on when you need the data.

They are usually enclosed with curly braces { }, with the key preceding the values.

Example #1:

>>>*myfriends = {"Paul": 35, "Dan": 26, "Lou": 28}*

>>>*myfriends = ["Lea"] = 40*

>>>*print (myfriends)*

{"Paul": 35, "Dan": 26, "Lou": 28, "Lea": 40}

Example #2:

You can add more key:value pairs, if you want, by following the process above:

>>>*{"Paul": 35, "Dan": 26, "Lou": 28, "Lea": 40}*

>>>*myfriends = ["Mandy": 23]*

>>> *print (myfriends)*

{"Paul": 35, "Dan": 26, "Lou": 28, "Lea": 40, "Mandy": 23}

Creating an empty dictionary

You can create an empty dictionary by using a pair of curly braces { }. You can add key:value pairs inside the curly braces to create initial key:value pairs. Remember to separate each pair with a comma. Be aware that their keys are also unique.

Example #1:

>>>*importantdays = {"birthday": 20, "graduation": 10, "marriage": 29}*

>>>*print (importantdays)*

{'birthday': 20, 'graduation': 10, 'marriage': 29}

Example #2:

>>>*mydates = {"Mom": 11, "Dad": 15, "Ned": 25, "Carla": 29}*

>>>*print (mydates)*

{'Mom': 11, 'Dad': 15, 'Ned': 25, 'Carla': 29}

You can use the dict() to create dictionaries directly from key:value pairs.

Example:

>>>*dict ([("Mom", 11), ("Dad", 15), ("Ned", 25), ("Carla", 29)])*

{'Mom': 11, 'Dad': 15, 'Ned': 25, 'Carla': 29}

Also, you can make use of arguments to create dictionaries.

Example:

>>>*dict ("Mom" = 11, "Dad" = 15, "Ned" = 25, "Carla" =29)*

{'Mom': 11, 'Dad': 15, 'Ned': 25, 'Carla': 29}

Deleting an entry from the dictionary

You can delete a key:value pair from dictionary by using the function 'del'.

Example:

>>>mydates = {"Mom": 11, "Dad": 15, "Ned": 25, "Carla": 29}

>>> del mydates ["Carla"]

>>>print (mydates)

{"Mom": 11, "Dad": 15, "Ned": 25}

Accessing and sorting keys from the dictionary

You can access all the keys from the dictionary by using the command:

list(d.keys( ))

This will display all the keys present in your dictionary.

Example:

>>>list(mydates.keys())

['Mom', 'Dad', 'Ned', 'Carla']

You can sort them out using the keyword for sorting data:

sorted.(d.keys( ))

Example:

>>>sorted(mydates.keys())

['Carla', 'Dad', 'Mom', 'Ned']

Finding specific keys

You can find specific keys by using the 'in' keyword.

Example #1:

>>>*"Carla" in mydates*

True

Example #2:

>>>*"Dennis" in mydates*

False

The dictionary is a source of significant resources. You can always call on the module help, when you can't seem to understand the terms. Know how to use the resources well, so that your Python experience will be a blast.

Chapter 13: More about Loops

Loops are imperative when you want to iterate elements or items in statements. In Python 3, you can execute the statements as many times as you want, sequentially.

This method is of great help in big organizations, where huge data have to be dealt with competently and repeatedly.

Using loops to enumerate values

for loops

You can enumerate values and find the indexes of the values simultaneously by using the function, enumerate( ). This is applicable most specifically in sequences.

Example:

>>>for i (index), v (value) in enumerate (['head', 'shoulders', 'knees', 'toes']) :

>>>print (i, v)

0 head

1 shoulders

2 knees

3 toes

Using loops to retrieve keys(k) and values(v) from dictionaries

You can use loops, while using the items method to retrieve keys and values from dictionaries.

Example:

> *>>>queens = {"Elizabeth": "the aristocrat", "Victoria" : "the Virgin", "Margaret": "the prudent", "Christina": "the pure"}*

> *>>>print (k, v)*

> *Elizabeth the aristocrat*

Victoria the Virgin

Margaret the prudent

Christina the pure

Using loops simultaneously over two or more sequences

You can use the zip function to perform this. You can do this by using the following syntax:

Example:

>>>*questions = ['church', 'school', 'room']*

>>>*answers = ('at the corner', 'behind the church', 'on the third floor')*

>>>*for q, a in zip (questions, answers) :*

>>>*print ("Where is the {0} ? It is {1}. ' .format (q, a))*

Output

Where is the church? It is at the corner.

Where is the school? It is behind the church.

Where is the room? It is on the third floor.

Using loops with 'while' statements

'While' statements are frequently used in looping. It breaks out the loop at some point when the statement is not true – several times. The Boolean expression (answerable by True or False) is used in this instance. Here how it is done.

Example:

>>> *x = 0*

>>> *while x ==6 :*

  x += 1

  print (x)

When you execute this code, the result would be:

7

```
>>>
```

It is done by adding 1 to the value that is equivalent to 6. Apparently, only 6 ==6. So, the loop stops at 6. When 1 is added, the answer is 7. The run stops at this point because all the rest of the numbers are not equal to 6.

You can break out of the while loop when the Boolean statement becomes False.

Example:

>>>condition = 1

1

>>>s= 0

0

>>>print ("Hello, type your number to get the sum.")

Hello, type your number to get the sum.

>>>print ("Type 0 to quit.")

Type 0 to quit.

>>>while condition != 0

print ("Sum: ", s)

x = float(input("Number: "))

s= s + condition

print ("Total: ", s)

This is what happens when you use the interactive IDLE interpreter. The return statement comes out immediately when you hit enter.

Hence, you may want to compose your code in the editor shell. So, you can edit it properly without being interrupted by prompt returns. See code below.

Example:

condition = 1

s = 0

print ("Hello, type your number to get the sum.")

print ("Type 0 to quit.")

while condition != 0

print ("Sum: ", s)

```
x = float(input("Number: "))

s= s + condition

print ("Total:  ", s)
```

You can now click run, and then run module in your Python shell. When the whole code is executed, the following will appear in your interactive shell:

Hello, type your number to get the sum.

Type 0 to quit.

Sum = 0

Number:

In the 'while' statement above, the user is being asked to input a number that the interpreter will add to any previous number to get the sum.

When a user types his number the sum will appear instantly below the word 'Number'.

For example, the user typed 13, the Python interpreter will compute and add this to the previous number to obtain the sum:

Hello, type your number to get the sum.

Type 0 to quit.

Sum = 0

Number: 13

13

This 'while' statement can run on and on, unless the user inputs 0, or the Boolean statement becomes False, (condition = 0), and not (condition != 0).

It is only when the code is executed, run or entered that the output would appear.

Example #2:

```
x = 2

while x > 2 :

print (x)

x = x += 2
```

In this example the loop will go on and on, as long as the value of x is more than 2. This would mean that the process will go on forever. The += signs signifies that 2 is added to the value of x. These are all control flow statements, generally used in loops. More will be discussed in the next chapter.

You can create an endless loop by using the statement:

> *While true:*
>
> *print ("hello")*

This is an infinite loop. It will print 'hello' until you break the loop. You can do this by typing control c, and the loop will break after a few seconds.

As you can see, Python codes can make life easier for anyone with its 'magical' commands that can create incredible apps in a snap. You have seen how a 4-line 'while' statement can create an endless addition capabilities of your Python shell.

Imagine this occurring in a larger scale, and you can appreciate the advantages of knowing the Python language.

Chapter 14: Using Control Flow Statements

Control flow tools are important in creating Python control flow statements and functions. These are tools that can assist you in manipulating your data, and are usually used with loops.

range ( ) function statements

This is a built-in function used in iterating a sequence of numbers.

Example #1: (for – in)

>>>*m = [0, 1, 2, 3, 4, 5, 6]*

>>>*for m in range (6):*

print (m)

0

1

2

3

4

5

If you have noticed, the end point of the range is not part of the resulting sequence. The range given is 6 but the result displayed is up to #5 only, albeit, the generated numbers are 6.

Therefore, if your range is: range (10), the return values are:

0

1

2

3

4

5

6

7

8

9

You have 10 values generated but the end point given is not included in the generated values.

You can also start the sequence at another number.

Example #1:

>>>range(4, 10):

The results will be the numbers or indices from 4 to 9)

Example #2:

>>> for x in range(6, 15):

[6, 7, 8, 9, 10, 11, 12, 13, 14]

These numbers may be presented in a vertical manner.

range ( ), len ( ) statements

You can use these statements to iterate the indices of a sequence.

Example:

>>>m = [0, 1, 2, 3, 4, 5, 6]

>>>for i in range(len(m)):

    if i % 3 == 1: continue

    print(m[i])

For statements

For statements are used to iterate the items in a list, in sequence.

Example #1:

>>>*names = ["Castro", "Fell", "Tebow", "Parker"]*

>>>*for "Fell" in names*

   print ("Fell")

'Fell'

if, elif, if-else statements

The if, elif, and if-else statements are considered as condition statements. A condition is set that has to be met.

<u>**if statement:**</u>

Example:

>>>*x = 15*

>>>*if x > 10*

   print ("improved")

improved   #output. "improved" was printed because the value of x is more

   than 10.

Let's use the previous example for if-else:

>>>*def len(x,y):*

>>> *If x < y:*

   return x:

  else:

   return y

break and continue statements

The break statement is usually used to stop or break loops (iterations), while the continue statement allows the loop's succeeding iteration to continue.

Example:

>>>names = ["Castro", "Fell', "Tebow", "Parker"]

>>>for name in "names"

    If name is =="Fell":

        break

>>>print ("current names: ", name)

If the condition is True, the break will occur. If the condition is False, there will be no break.

The execution of the command will continue in the next immediate statement following the loop.

Reminders:

- After the loop statement, white spaces (4 spaces) must be follow before the next entry. The next input should follow the indentation if it's part of the loop statement. However, Python has already remedied this by automatically adjusting the interpreter's indentation, without you doing it. If the statement is not part of the loop statement, you can adjust the indentation to the original.

    Example:

    >>>def len(x,y):

    >>> If x < y:

        return x: #This should be indented 4 spaces

    else:

        return y #This should be indented 4 spaces

But don't worry, Python did it for you, as soon as it senses the loop statements, it adjusts accordingly when you hit enter.

Chapter 15: Defining Functions

You can define a function by using the keyword def. You can use the general code syntax: def function_name():

General code syntax

def function_name (parameter or argument list):

statements (indented)

A return statement will end the execution of the code, and it can consist of one or more returns, depending on the Python script or code that you have inputted.

Example #1:

```
>>>def grams(w_in_milligrams):
    """"returns the weight in grams""""
        return(w_in_milligrams / 1000)
        for w in (500, 250, 100, 245, 320, 40, 432):
>>>print (w, ":  ", grams, (w))
```

When you hit execute, run or enter, the output will be:

milligrams grams

500 :   0.500

250 :   0.250

100 :   0.100

245 :   0.245

320 :   0.320

40 :   0.040

432 :   0.432

The output above is based on the fact that 1,000 mg (milligrams) is == to 1 g (gram).

In addition, you can define functions making use of the combination of three forms: keyword arguments, default arguments values, and arbitrary argument lists.

Keyword arguments

The kwarg=value form can also be used to call functions. The parameters (param) identify the arguments (arg).

Example:

>>>*def printdata (str)*

>>>*def printdata (name, state) :*

"This prints the data into this function"

    print ("Name: ", name)

    print ("State: ", state)

    printdata (name = "Walters", state = "Washington")

    return

Output:

Name: Walters

State: Washington

Default argument values

These are usually used only once to call a function. These are arguments that assume default values for arguments that don't have values that are provided in the function call.

Example:

>>>*def printdata (str)*

>>>*def printdata (gender, age = 40) :*

"This prints the data into this function"

    print ("Gender: ", gender)

    print ("Age: ", age)

    printdata (gender = "female")

    return

When you execute the code, this will be the return statement:

Gender : female

Age 40

The age has taken the default value of the call function, which is 40.

Arbitrary argument lists

You can call this function making use of a number of arguments. Furthermore, you can make function calls using keyword parameters. But these parameters must not be used as positional arguments.

The general code for this type of function is:

>>>*def functionName ([formal_args,] * var_args_tuple) :*

Example:

>>>*def state (**args) :*

    print (args)

    state()

    { }

>>>*state(WY="Wyoming", AL="Alabama", AK="Alaska")*

{'AK' : 'Alaska', 'WY' : 'Wyoming', 'AL' : 'Alabama'}

Defining or creating your own functions

You can define your own functions too. The general Python code is:

>>>def func() :

The colon after the statement denotes that the statement has ended. After the function statement, you can also input another function/statement in the body of the code.

This is how you can define your own functions:

1. State the function keyword, def, followed by the name of your function.

    Example:

    >>>*def functionname*

2. Next, after the function name, insert an open parenthesis and write your argument/s, and add a closing parenthesis, and then a colon. Don't forget this important step.

    Example:

    >>>*def functionname(arg) :*

3. Next, add your Python statements that you want to run.

    Example:

    >>>*def functionname(arg) :*
    statement 1
    statement 2

    When you press 'enter' once, the prompt arrows will still not appear because the interpreter is waiting for you to enter or input another statement.

    If you press 'enter' twice, the interpreter will understand that you're done with the statements, and the prompt arrows will then appear.

4. Now, you may want to add the print() statement or the return statement, whichever you prefer.

   Example:

   ```
   >>>def functionname(arg) :
           statement 1
           statement 2
           print (functionname)
   ```

Let's say you want a function in classifying a set of items, whether they are True or False, and you named it TF.

Example #1:

```
>>>def TF(x):

        if x == 'True':

        print (x, "is correct")

        else:

        print (x, "is wrong")
```

Example #2:

```
>>>def func() :

        print ("Python is cool!")

        print ("I love Python.")

        print ("See you around.")


>>>func ()

Python is cool!

I love Python.

See you around.

>>>
```

Example #3:

>>>def func2(a, b, c) :

    return a + b + c

When you call func2 anew, with values assigned to your parameters, the interpreter will solve the math equation automatically, when you press enter. See example below:

>>>def func2(101, 215, 328)

644

>>>

or

>>>def func2(a, b, c)

    print ("a= ", a, "b = ", b, "c= ", c)

Thus, if you call the function, and you assign values, this will be the return statement:

>>>func2(2, 4, 6) #These are the values that you are assigning to a, b, c.

a = 2 b = 4 c = 6

You have to assign values to each parameter. If you don't, an error will occur. If you cannot assign values, you can use a default value for the last two parameters. The first parameter must always have an assigned value.

All you have to do is to insert the values after the parameter in the def function statement.

Example:

>>>def func2(a, b=3, c=4)

    print ("a= ", a, "b = ", b, "c= ", c)

Based on the code above, you can simply assign a value to 'a', and the rest will be the default value.

Example:

>>>*func2(2)*

a = 2 b = 3 c= 4 #All the values appeared even if you have inputted one

only, because you have already assigned the default

values.

When you assign values to the parameters, ensure that there are corresponding values to all of the arguments or parameters. If you don't, you will be obtaining return errors.

The ability to create user-defined functions will allow you to create functions that you specifically require for your data or files. The advantage is that you create the code only once, but you can use it for as long as you want.

If you want some modifications in the code, you can quickly modify it, according to your preferences. No sweat!

Your user-defined functions will be an essential aspect of the smooth manipulation of your Python files.

Use it to your own advantage.

Chapter 16: Lambda Function in Python 3

The lambda function/ operator in Python 3 is a one-line function that does not use def and return, as commonly done in Python. Hence, it's simpler and easier to use.

This function is a short, anonymous one, generally used with reduce( ), filter( ), and maps( ). If you prefer it, the list comprehension' can also be used.

General statement for lambda function

The general statement in using the lambda function is:

>   *lambda argument_list: expression*

The arguments are separated by commas, and the expression is a math expression.

Example #1:

In adding a and b variables using lambda, your syntax will be:

>   *>>>sum = lambda x, y: x + y*

>   *>>>sum = (5,8)*

>   *13*

The traditional Python syntax is:

>   *>>>def add x, y:*

>   *>>>return x + y*

List comprehension for the same statement:

>   *>>>print (x +y)*

Example #2:

The lambda operator can also be used in 'if - else' statements.

>>>len = lambda x, y:x if x is <y x else y

>>>print (len(3,9))

If you use the traditional method, it would be a longer statement:

>>>def len(x,y):

>>> If x < y:

　return x:

　else:

　return y

>>>print (len(3,9))

In the statement above, we have the length of the variables x and y. We want to obtain only values that are lesser than x. So, if the value is lesser than x, it will appear in the returns, if not, the value of y will appear.

Obviously, the lambda statement or code is shorter, and can be stated using one-liner statements only.

The list comprehension statement for example #2, which is shown above:

>>>print ([x for x in len if x < y])

Filter function

This function filters out items in a sequence to create a new list by using conditions. Thus, the filter function has to have the first argument as a function (f), with a Boolean return value (True or False). This is applied to each element in the list.

Example: (using lambda operator)

>>>num = [3,6,10]

>>>print (list(filter(lambda x:x<10, num)))

[3,6]

In the example above, the argument is that if x is lesser than 10, num (number) will appear in the results.

Undoubtedly, the lambda makes life easier for Python coders.

Reduce function

The reduce function is responsible in reducing a list to a single value. However, this function has been dropped from Python 3.

The lambda function and the list reduction methods make Python statements shorter, but equally reliable as a programming language.

Chapter 17: Modules and Packages and Their Functions

You should learn how to arrange your files (classes, function and variables) into an organized filing system. You can create your own, or use the builtin modules.

What are modules?

You can organize your files using modules. Modules are groups of data that you can refer and retrieve promptly when required. These can contain some Python codes that you needed at that moment.

What are packages?

Packages are like folders. They contain two or more modules, which are organized properly. They use the __init__.py file name (empty file).

Using modules

To use modules, you have to import them first. You can import them using this code:

>>>*import module_name*

When you use the module, you have to use the general code/statement:

>>>*module_name.function*

You can also directly call for it with this code:

>>>*from module_name import function*

You can then use the function.

>>>*function()*

This will return the value, and not an error.

Two ways in importing packages

Absolute import

You can use absolute import with any of these general codes:

> *import package.module*
>
> *obj = package.module.ClassA()*

> *from package.module import Class A()*
>
> *import ClassA()*

> *from package import module*
>
> *obj =module.ClassA()*

> *>>>from module_name import**

#This statement will import all of the modules because of the asterisk. However, you will encounter problems, if there are duplicate modules. These are modules with the same names.

Relative imports

You can import the class of one module to another module in the same package. Use the code below.

Example of Python code:

> *from.module1 import ClassA*
>
> *obj = ClassA()*

Example #2:

> *from..module2 import ClassB*
>
> *obj = ClassB()*

Dates and Time

There are two types of Date and Times objects. These are 'naïve' and 'aware. Times and dates are reliably done through the datetime module.

The difference between the two types is that 'aware' is aware of its 'environment', regarding the time zone, necessary time adjustments and similar aspects of the time it exists in.

On the other hand, 'naïve' – just as the term implies – is naïve of its 'environment'. It doesn't contain ample information to operate on its own. It has to be dependent on the device's program.

The datetime module contains the timezone class (UTC). We have also the time.time function, which can provide the date and time in ticks or seconds. It can be complex for beginners, so I will try to present it in the simplest manner.

Not all topics will be covered and discussed. The more advanced data about this topic are not included.

The following are the constants that are exported by the datetime module:

datetime.MINYEAR

This is equivalent to 1. This indicates that the returns will include the years way, way back, even during the years that Python was still not in existence. It's the smallest amount of year provided by a date object or a datetime object.

>>>*datetime.time = datetime.time(hours=0, minute=0) :*

If you want to extract or obtain the current time, you can use these codes:

Example #1:

>>>*import datetime*

>>>*current_time = datetime.datetime.now()*

>>>*print ("{:%H:%M}".format(current_time))*

11:28

Example #2:

>>>*import datetime*

>>>*datetime.datetime.now()*

>>>*print(now.year)*

2016

Example #3

>>>*import datetime*

>>>*datetime.datetime.now()*

>>>*print (time.localtime())*

11:28

Or

>>>*import datetime*

>>>*print ("Local Current time : ", localtime)*

11:28

datetime.MAXYEAR

This is equivalent to 9999. This maximum range ensures that scores of years will pass until the method or function becomes obsolete or ineffective. It's the largest amount of year provided by a date object or a datetime object.

Classes related to datetime module

There are classes related to your datetime module. These are:

datetime.datetime – as specified, this class combines the date and time including the smallest time measurement, which is microseconds. In addition, the seconds, minutes, hours, days, months and year are also provided. Information provided by the tzinfo subclass can provide the UTC time offsets.

datetime.date – this class provides the year, month and day based on the Gregorian calendar.

datetime.tzinfo – this class allows the adjustment of time according to the programs preferences. An example is when you want to adjust the time to be in congruence with the daylight-saving time and timezone. Thus, it acts as an abstract that you can promptly call, whenever necessary.

datetime.timezone – this class is utilized to implement the changes made by datetime.tzinfo and present it as a fixed offset from the UTC.

datetime.timedelta – this class expresses the time difference between datetime or date, time events, and is expressed in the smallest time measurement, which is microseconds.

> There are time.delta objects that you must be familiar with. The essential fact to remember is this object indicates the difference between two sets of dates and times, the least time duration is in microseconds (1,000 of a millisecond).

> When creating your Python code for time.delta, keep in mind that it's your choice to include arguments or not. Take note too that arguments are given 0 as a default value.

datetime.time – this class is similar to datetime.datetime, only it does not include the year, month and day but only the time in hours, minutes, seconds, microseconds and tzinfo.

Time module

In versions of the Python 3 series, this time module can provide various methods to obtain the data or function you need with regards to time (Windows and Unix). Take note that epoch is the point when the time starts. Obviously, that would be equivalent to zero.

This topic may be too complicated for beginners; therefore, we will discuss only the most commonly use methods. You can always continue to learn about the rest as you go along with your learning process.

Most common methods used for time module

1. **time.clock( )**

This returns the time in seconds, with the value expressed as floats. You can use time.clock for various purposes.

Example:

> >>>import time
> >>>def procedure() :

2. time.sleep(t in secs)

This is the duration of time in seconds that the clock suspends its operation. As the term implies, time 'sleeps'; it takes a nap for a few minutes or seconds.

Example:

> >>>import time
> >>>print ("Start : %s" % time.ctime())
> Start : Wed Dec 21 3:23:15 2016 #output
> >>>time.sleep(10)
> >>>print ("End : %s" % time.ctime())
> End : Wed Dec 21 3:23:25 2016 #output

3. time.ctime([secs])

This converts time to localtime. The conversion is in seconds.

Example:

> >>>import time
> >>>print ("ctime : ", time.ctime())
> ctime : Wed Dec 21 3:36:20 2016 #output or result

4. time.time()

This returns the current time in seconds (UTC) since the epoch (0). The time noted would be the last time you have called the method.

Example:

>>>*import time*
>>>*print ("time.time : % f", % time.time())*
Time.time() = #This will give the values in seconds in a floating
point

5. time.localtime([secs])

This method is handy in converting the number of seconds to local time. You may want this method, when you happen to be in another locale at any given time.

Example:

>>>*import time*
>>>*print ("time.localtime() : %s" , time.localtime())*
#This command will print the time in local time.

6. time.tzset( )

This method resets the time based on timezone variables.   Use this properly to ensure that there are no errors in the time obtained.

Example:

>>>*import time or datetime*
>>>*def reset_tz() :*
>>>   *os.environ('TZ') = 'UTC'*
>>>   *time.tzset()*
>>>*print ((time.strftime('%X %x %Z'))*
#The return will be the re-set time.

7. time.gmtime([secs])

This method converts the time in seconds to a structured time (struc_time) in UTC. This is becoming popular because of its reliability.

8. time.strftime(format[, t])

This method converts a struc_time or tuple to gmtime or local time. There are symbols or codes that are used with time.strftime that you may not be familiar with.

106

9. time.struc_time

There are common symbols or strf (string format) directives that you can usually encounter, when dealing with datetime modules.

This object has a TimeTuple or a tuple interface that handles time with 9 numbers.

Index	Attributes	Values or Ranges
0	year (4 digits)	2016
1	month	1 to 12
2	day	1 to 31
3	hour	0 to 23
4	minute	0 to 59
5	second	0 to 61
6	weekday	0 to 6; Monday is 0
7	day of year	1 to 366 Julian day
8	daylight savings	library determines DST

Basic codes and their meanings

%d = day of the month expressed in decimal numbers. Take note that 0 is the starting number, applicable to single digit-numbers. Know the difference between this code and %-d.

%-d = day of the month expressed as decimal numbers; the range is from 1 to 31. These numbers correspond to the days of the month, such as Jan 1, Jan 2 up to Jan 31. Likewise, it is applicable to the other months.

%x = date of locale, represented by month/day/year (12/21/2016). If the numbers correspond to single digits.

Example: Let's say for example, January 1, 2017, the format would be:

01/01/2017

%X = time of locale, presented by hour:minutes:seconds.

Example:

06:17:02 (6 hours; 17 minutes; 2 seconds)

%c = date and time of locale, presented by day, month, date, time (hour:minutes:seconds), year.

Example:

Wed Dec 21 06:17:02 2016

%z = time zone for UTC offset, presented by +HHMM or -HHMM forms. When you use this form, double check the entries to avoid errors; you can easily commit errors.

%M = minutes expressed with 0 if single-digit. (01, 02, 03, ...). Take note that there's also a small m that has another meaning.

%-M = minutes that can be expressed in decimal numbers. (1, 2, 3, ...)

%m = month presented with 0, if single digit. It ranges from 1 to 12. (01, 02, 03, ...)

%-m = month presented in decimal numbers. It ranges from 1 to 12 but occurs as is. (1, 2, 3, ...). You don't pad it with 0.

%a = abbreviated name of weekday, Mon, Tue, Wed, Thu, Fri, Sat, Sun. This is preferred over %A because the names used are brief and can be promptly inserted.

%A = full name of weekday, Monday, Tuesday, Wednesday, Thursday, Friday, Saturday, Sunday based on locale.

%w = weekday starting with Sunday as 0. It follows that Monday is 1, Tuesday is 2, Wednesday is 3, Thursday is 4, Friday is 5, and Saturday is 6.

%b = month's abbreviated name (locale), Jan, Feb, Mar, Apr, May, Jun, Jul, Aug, Sep, Oct, Nov, Dec. This form is used more by coders because of their brevity.

%B = month's full name (locale), January, February, March, April, May, June, July, August, September, October, November, December.

%y = year without century. It just displays the last two digits. See examples below.

Examples:

> *16*
>
> *For 2016*
>
> *17*
>
> *for 2017*

%Y = Year with century.

Examples:

> *2016*
>
> *2017*

%p = indicates whether AM or PM (locale)

%I = hours, based on the 12-hour clock. Zero is added before the number for single digit numbers.

Examples:

> *01, 02, 03, 04, 05, 06, 07, 08, 09, 10, 11, 12*

%-I = hours, based on the 12-hour clock. Presented as is:

Examples:

> *1, 2, 3, 4, 5, 6, 7, 8, 9, 10 11, 12*

%H = hours, based on the 24-hour clock. Zero is added before single digit numbers; the zero adds as a pad to present a two-digit number.

Examples:

01, 02, 03, 04, 05, 06, 07, 08, 09, 10, 11, 12, 13, 14, 15, 16, 17, 18, 19, 20, 21,

22, 23, 24

01:20

%-H = hours, based on the 24-hour clock and are presented as is.

Examples:

1, 2, 3, 4, 5, 6, 7, 8, 9, 10 11, 12, 13, 14, 15, 16, 17, 18, 19, 20, 21, 22, 23, 24

1:20

%S = seconds, with single-digit numbers presented with zero.

Examples:

01, 02, 03, ...

%-S = seconds, presented as is, and as decimal numbers.

Examples:

1, 2, 3, ...

%f = microseconds in decimal numbers, 000000. You can use this whenever

needed.

%j = day of the year, based on the 365 days of the year. It can be expressed as a decimal number.

%-j = day of the year as decimal number, based on the 365 days of the year.

%U = week number of the year, expressed as decimal numbers. There are roughly 91 weeks in a year, starting with week 0. In this method, Sunday is the first day of the week. Likewise, it can be considered as the first week number of the year.

%W = week number of the year, expressed as decimal points. Based on the number of weeks in a year, in which Monday is considered as the first day of the week. This is true in this particular method.

Hopefully, these codes could help you understand more how the Python syntax for datetime were created. When you read these complex codes, it can be daunting at first, but you can try practicing with some of the dates, and you will get the hang of it eventually.

Reminders:

- Keep in mind that datetime is a module that you can import to help you access dates and times. Maximize its use.

- You can format your date and time using this simple method: '{:%Y-%m-%d %H:%M}'

    Example:

    '{:%Y-%m-%d %H:%M}'.format(datetime(2016, 12, 21, 6, 5,))
    #This indicates that the datetime will be formatted as 2016 − 12 − 21, 06:05

- It's recommended to adjust your time to locale time, so you will be truly aware of the 'real' time around you.

- Always consider the environment that the time is existing in, when adjusting the time.

Chapter 18: Creating Input Programs in Python

Creating programs in Python 3 is similar to Python 2's processes. You have to save your file every time you're done because Python does not save it automatically. You have to do it yourself.

The 'input' code is one of the most commonly used program in Python. It requires the user to participate in the process because the user has to 'input' a certain data for the program to continue.

Steps in creating the input program

Step #1 – Open your editor

IDLE is Python's interactive shell, where you can type your codes. From your downloaded Python 3, open your shell and click New Window, and then New File. This will prompt another shell to appear. This shell is the editor and is not interactive. You can press enter and continue typing your code, without the shell interpreting your code prematurely.

This is advantageous for beginner's because most often, they commit mistakes. Don't worry, though. As a beginner, you are expected to commit mistakes. Consider your mistakes as stepping stones to your learning process.

Step #2 – Write your input program

You can write whatever your program you want. In this particular case, it's an input program. Your input program can be simply written this way:

>>>*input() or* >>>*input("Name: ")*

When you press enter in your interactive Python shell, this will appear:

Name:

You have to type your name.

Name: Michael

Michael

Step #3 - Save your new file

Before you run your Python code, you have first to save it because your code will be deleted as soon as you close the shell. Simply click 'Save As' to save your file. Take note that it should be a .py file. You may want to save it in a place that is easily accessible from your computer.

Step #4 – Run your code

You can now run your code repeatedly, as long as you have saved it. You can assign a variable (for example x) for your input program.

You could also modify it later, when you want to change some aspects of your code.

Sample codes

Example #1:

```
x = input ("Name:  ")
print (x)
```

Example #2:

```
>>>input ("Age:  ")
    print (x)
```

Since the answer is definitely a number, you may want to indicate in your code that the value is an integer.

```
>>> int (inpul("Age:  "))
    print (x)
```

Another way is to convert the integer to a string. It's because the input value is always a string.

To convert an integer to a string, use this code:

str()

Examples:

str(5)

str(10)

The above numbers will then be converted to strings, so they can now operate as strings.

Python coding style

The correct coding style will prevent you from obtaining return errors in your codes. Proper grammar or syntax is of utmost importance. Here are some coding styles that are most preferred by Python.

1. Comments should be written (as much as possible) in another line from the code. The usual practice of commenting after every line of code is popular nowadays. Even so, writing comments on another line is recommended. This is because beginners, not familiar with the hash # symbol, will mistake the comment as part of the code.

2. Python's UTF-8 and plain ASCII are preferred to be used as codes. There are changes as Python is updated frequently to solve snags or problems.

3. In naming functions, classes and arguments, Python has a preferred style. Functions are named using the lowercase or with underscores. Classes are named using the CamelCase. In the case of arguments, the first argument always uses 'self'.

4. Remember to add spaces around operators and after commas. This is a good practice because the statement can be read clearly and it would appear organized.

5. Larger block of codes, blank lines and classes should be separated by white spaces. Unlike other programming languages, Python has made it possible for users not to worry so much about these white spaces. They have been added as part of the program.

6. If your device has no builtin indentation, don't use the tabs in adding spaces. This may create a problem. It's better to use a 4-space indentation than using the tab.

7. Lines should not exceed 79 characters; thus, you have to wrap text properly. A problem occurs when the lines exceed 79 characters. The code may not work.

8. In using Python, docstrings are preferred because they are easier to manipulate and are practical.

You can create different types of programs with your Python language. Explore your codes and be ingenious to learn more coding best practices.

Chapter 19: Practice Questions on Coding

This chapter is devoted for your coding practice. I will give you a case and you decide what Python code should you use to obtain the objective. Keep in mind that there are several ways to skin a cat, so choose the best method or function that can answer the question. Good luck!

Here goes:

Questions or cases

Instruction:

Answer the questions in the following cases. If needed, write the Python code of your answer.

1. You are a group leader for a research study. You want to sort your Python file showing the names of the subjects in alphabetical order. What Python code/statement should you use?

2. In Python, what would be the quickest way to get the sum of numbers? Show the statement.

1. How can you write the code, if you want to add 14 to this list of myNumbers?
   myNumbers = [2, 4, 6, 8, 10, 12]

3. How can you remove duplicate elements from this set?

   names = {"John", "Ella", "Judith", "Jonathan", "John", "Eliot" }

4. How can you retrieve elements 2 to 6 from this list?

   myVariables = (1, 2, 3, 4, 5, 6, 7)

5. The employees in your company needed to register their names before a social gathering, using Python. What program would you employ? Give the details of your program/code.

6. Write a function that would allow you to use 'treatment' as a variable in an a + b situation.

7. Create a while statement, if x = 1.

8. Create an if-else statement concerning working hours of employees under your supervision. They must input their number of working hours.

9. Solve this problem using Python. 7 raised to the 5th power, multiplied by 10 and added to 1,230.

10. How do you write the Python code if you want the following to appear on your return statements:

    Hello!

    I'm having a great time writing my Python code.

    Would you like to join me?

    Enter your name now

    Name:

After answering the questions, review your answers one more time before referring to the answers in the next chapter.

You can now turn to the next page to check your answers.

Chapter 20: Answers to Practice Questions on Coding

Here are the answers to the questions in the previous chapter. Go over them and compare your answers. Again, there may be other methods to create your code. They may not be given all in the answers. Refer to the chapters in this book too to confirm your answers.

Questions and answers

1. You are a group leader for a research study. You want to sort your Python file showing the surnames of the subjects (file name = employees_name) in alphabetical order. What Python code/statement would you use?
   employees_name = ("Lobo", "Anden", "Guillermo", "Dixon", "Henry")

   Answer:

   Use the sorted data by calling the function, sorted () . The Python code would be:

   ```
   >>> employees_name = ("Lobo", "Anden", "Guillermo", "Dixon", "Henry")
   >>> sorted (employees_name)
   >>>print (employees_name)
   'Anden', 'Dixon', 'Guillermo', 'Henry', 'Lobo'
   ```

   You could also use:

   ```
   >>>employees_name.sort
   >>>print (employees_name)
   'Anden', 'Dixon', 'Guillermo', 'Henry', 'Lobo'
   ```

2. In Python, what would be the quickest way to get the sum of two numbers, with these values: a = 5, b = 10? Show the statement.

   Answer:

   ```
   >>> a = 5, b = 10

   >>> a + b
   15
   ```

   a = is the 1st number
   b = is the 2nd number

You can also use the Python interpreter as a calculator and input the numbers directly to get the sum.

Example:

```
>>> 5 + 10
15
```

Or

```
>>>a + b
15
```

3. How can you write the code, if you want to add 14 to this list of myNumbers?
   myNumbers = [2, 4, 6, 8, 10, 12]

   Answer:

   ```
   >>>myNumbers = [2, 4, 6, 8, 10, 12]
   >>> myNumbers .append (14)
   >>>print (myNumbers)
   myNumbers = [2, 4, 6, 8, 10, 12, 14]
   ```

4. How can you remove duplicate elements from this set?

   names = {"John", "Ella", "Judith", "Jonathan", "John", "Eliot"}

   Answer:

   There are various ways to do it, one of the simplest methods is this:

   ```
   >>>def remove_duplicates(names):
        return list(set(names))
   ```

   You can also turn it into a set to weed out duplicates.

5. How can you retrieve elements 2 to 6 from this list?

   myList = [1, 2, 3, 4, 5, 6, 7]

   Answer:

```
>>> myList = [1, 2, 3, 4, 5, 6, 7]
>>> print [2:7]
2, 3, 4, 5, 6
```

6. The employees in your company needed to register their nicknames before a social gathering, using Python. What program would you employ? Give the details of your program/code.

Answer:

First, you have to create the Python code and save it in your device before running. You can write the code in this manner:

>>>print ("What is your nickname?")

>>>print ("Enter your nickname.")

>>>input("nickname: ")

>>>print ("Thank you. Enjoy the party!")

>>>print (nickName)

When you run this code, the following will be the output:

What is your nickname?

Enter your nickname.

nickname:

Thank, you enjoy the party!

_____ (Python will print your nickname here.)

7. Write a function that would allow you to use 'treatment' as a variable in an a + b situation.

Answer:

>>>treatment1 = ("daily", "weekly", "monthly")
>>>treatment2 = ("short", 'medium", "long")

```
>>>a = "treatment1"
>>>b = "treatment2"
>>> a + b
treatment1, treatment2
```

or

```
>>>treatment1 + treatment2
```

"daily", "weekly", "monthly", short", 'medium", "long"

8. Create a while statement, if x = 20.

   Answer:

   ```
   x = 20
   >>>while x >5
           print (x)
   ```

   This will print numbers from 6 to 20 because they are all greater than 5.

9. Create an if-else statement concerning working hours of employees under your supervision. They must input their number of working hours.

   Answer:

   ```
   >>>x = 2
   >>>print ("Kindly type your working hours below.")
   >>> int(input("working hours:  "))
   >>> if x < 8
           print ("Work harder.")
       else
           print ("Take it easy.")
   ```

When you run this code, the output would be:

   Kindly type your working hours below.
   working hours:

When the employee types his working hours and it's less than 8 hours the comment "Work harder" will appear. When the working hours is more than 8 hours, the comment: "Take it easy." will appear.
See output below:

   Kindly type your working hours below.

working hours: 6
Work harder.

Or

Kindly type your working hours below.
working hours: 9
Take it easy.

10. Solve this problem using Python.
7 raised to the 5th power, multiplied by 10 and added to 1,230.

Answer:

>>>(7**5) * 10 + 1,230
169, 300

The exponent is solved first, even if it's not enclosed in parentheses. Then the answer is multiplied with 10, and then added to 1,230.

7**5 = 16, 807
16, 807 x 10 = 168, 070
168, 070 + 1,230 = 169, 300

11. How do you write the Python code if you want the following to appear on your return statements:

Hello!

I'm having a great time writing my Python code.

Would you like to join me?

Enter your name now

Name:

Answer:

print ("Hello!")

print ("I'm having a great time writing my Python code.")

print ("Would you like to join me?")

print ("Enter your name now")

```
input ("Name:  ")
```

Click 'run module' for the return statements to be printed. This was constructed in the shell editor, so the arrow prompts are not seen. You will be obtaining the same results:

Hello!

I'm having a great time writing my Python code.

Would you like to join me?

Enter your name now

Name:

There you go!

If you have other answers other than these answers, that's fine. It means you have learned something. As the cliché goes: "There are several ways to reach the top of the mountain."

Mine is not the only way. The important thing is to remember the basic Python rules that you should follow.

Chapter 21: Basic Tips to Remember in Python 3 Programming

As we end the lessons, here are important tips that you should remember about the Python 3 programming language. Go over them and apply them properly.

1. **Learn with the correct attitude.** With your mind positively prepared to assimilate new information, your learning will be more productive and enjoyable.

2. **Python 3 has still many similarities with Python 2.** If you know Python 2 already, it would be easier for you to learn Python 3; the changes are not astronomical.

3. **Maximize the builtin functions**. If you encounter problems in constructing your codes, search for builtin functions that can help you solve the problem. All you have to do is to call on the function to direct you.

4. **Be brave to explore, while learning**. Experiment with your codes. You may commit mistakes along the way, but you will learn from your adventure. Of course, ensure that you have saved a copy first of your data before you start tweaking them.

5. **Remember print ().** This is the most common function that you must remember for Python 3. Print has become a function, so it needs the parentheses to enclose items for printing. Without the parentheses, a return error will occur. Python 2 works, whether the parentheses are used or not.

6. **Python is a new language.** As a beginner, you may find Python difficult. It's like learning the ABCs of a foreign language. There's no shame in learning at your own pace. Slowly but surely, you will achieve your goal.

7. **Numbers are not enclosed in quotes**. Unlike text, numbers included in the data types are typically not enclosed in quotes. They are included in data files as they are.

8. **Use a reliable Python interactive interpreter**. IDLE works on various OS and is reliable and easy to manipulate.

9. **Lists are mutable, while numbers, tuples, and strings are immutable.** You must remember these facts, because it can help you in

creating a correct Python syntax. Mixing up your marks will mess up your files too.

10. **Think like a computer.** The codes will be easier to remember if you psyche yourself to think as a computer. How does the computer operate? It saves, deletes, creates, add and manipulate files. Observe how it processes data, and learn from it. An example is when you close a file, the computer will always remind you to save it. Your mind must also be attuned to these 'reminders'.

11. **Interact with other coders**. You may want to join an online group or a neighborhood group of programmers or coders. Your interactions with them will allow you to acquire new knowledge through their experiences, while sharing your own. This can be offline or online. It doesn't matter, provided that you have a good relationship.

12. **Remember the correct punctuation marks that go together with the various data types**. Sets and the dictionary use curly brackets. Lists and tuples use brackets; strings and variables use parentheses.

13. **Be aware of the Python operators**. The operators are vital in creating a correct syntax. Review the operators presented in this book, and remember their functions. You will need them to become a great Python coder.

14. **Python recognizes other Control Flow Statements**. The Control Flow Statements of other programming languages are recognized by Python. It's amazing, isn't it? If you happen to know other programming languages, you will find Python to be relatively easy.

15. **Learn about other programming languages.** You may want to study JAVA, JavaScript, HTML and CSS. They have many similarities that will facilitate your education. When you have knowledge about all of these, you can turn it into a career and become an expert language programmer.

16. Practice, practice, practice. Practice makes perfect. If you want to be an expert in language programming. Practice coding every chance you get. Your diligence will, inevitably, pay off in the long run.

17. **Update yourself regularly.** Python has evolved throughout the years. It's best to update yourself, every now and then, to know which recent features are added to its current apps.

18. **When choosing a Python code, go with the simplest**. The goal of a language programmer is to accomplish his task through the easiest way possible. So, always choose the simplest method. Obviously, it needs to be reliable, as well.

19. **Python is free.** You can download all the updated versions of Python for free. You don't pay a cent, yet, you can gain tremendous benefits from learning this programming language.

These tips will enrich your Python experience. Consider them as guidelines in your journey to gain knowledge.

Observe them, and you will be a happy Python coder and programmer.

Conclusion

You have now a beginner's knowledge about Python 3. Practicing with your codes every day can help you retain and apply the basics that you have gleaned from this book.

Pursue more advance knowledge, while your Python basics are still intact and fresh in your mind. Understandably, advance users have more advantage over beginners in terms of speed and expertise. But you're going there, slowly but surely.

For as long as you are motivated to learn, you will be able to continue and pursue advance lessons in Python.

Take note that 'knowledge applied is knowledge gained'. Thus, don't sit on your laurels yet. Go out there, and try your hands on more actual Python coding.

As you start coding, you will discover the joy of creating, manipulating, organizing and working on your own files. It can be an exhilarating experience.

Again, congratulations and welcome to the world of Python 3!

www.ingramcontent.com/pod-product-compliance
Lightning Source LLC
Chambersburg PA
CBHW080556060326
40689CB00021B/4870

* 9 7 8 1 5 4 2 4 6 1 2 5 2 *